RELIABILITY STATISTICS

Reliability Statistics

Robert A. Dovich

Library of Congress Cataloging-in-Publication Data

Dovich, Robert A.
    Reliability statistics / Robert A. Dovich.
      p. cm.
    Includes bibliographical references.
    1. Reliability (Engineering) — Statistical methods. I. Title.
  TA169.D686 1990
  620'.00452 — dc20

90-35282
CIP

ISBN 0-87389-086-8

1098765

Acquisitions editor: Jeanine L. Lau.
Production editor: Tammy Griffin
Cover design by Artistic License.
Set in Times by DanTon Typographers. Printed and bound by BookCrafters.

American Society for Quality

Quality Press
611 East Wisconsin Avenue
Milwaukee, Wisconsin 53201-3005
800-248-1946
Web site http://www.asq.org

In memory of Becky

Without whose support and assistance,
this book would not have been possible.

CONTENTS

PREFACE

The purpose of this book is to provide a significant amount of the statistical applications used by both quality and reliability engineering personnel in the performance of their duties. With this in mind, the book is applications oriented rather than theoretical in nature, and does not require mathematical skills beyond algebra and elementary statistical methods.

The bibliography contains references that were useful in researching the material for this book, and will provide the reader with a broader-based understanding of the fields of reliability and maintainability engineering.

This book can serve as a handy reference for those needing a quick reference to the material contained herein, as well as those preparing for the Certified Reliability Engineer (CRE) and Certified Quality Engineer (CQE) exams.

RELIABILITY DEFINITIONS — MIL-STD-721

DEFINITION OF TERMS FOR RELIABILITY AND MAINTAINABILITY ▮▮▮▮▮▮▮▮▮▮

Accessibility A measure of the relative ease of admission to the various areas of an item for the purpose of operation or maintenance.

Availability A measure of the degree to which an item is in the operable and commitable state at the start of the mission, when the mission is called for at an unknown (random) time.

Burn-in The operation of an item under stress to stabilize its characteristics.

Capability A measure of the ability of an item to achieve mission objectives given the conditions during the mission.

Checkout Tests or observations of an item to determine its condition or status.

Debugging A process to detect and remedy inadequacies.

Demonstrated That which has been measured by the use of objective evidence gathered under specified conditions.

Dependability A measure of the degree to which an item is operable and capable of performing its required function at any (random) time during a specified mission profile, given item availability at the start of the mission.

Derating	(a) Using an item in such a way that applied stresses are below rated values, or
	(b) The lowering of the rating of an item in one stress field to allow an increase in rating in another stress field.
Durability	A measure of useful life (a special case of reliability).
Failure	The event, or inoperable state, in which an item or part of an item does not, or would not, perform as previously specified.
Failure analysis	Subsequent to a failure, the logical systematic examination of an item, its construction, application, and documentation to identify the failure mode and determine the failure mechanism and its basic course.
Failure, dependent	Failure which is caused by the failure of an associated item(s). Not independent.
Failure, independent	Failure which occurs without being caused by the failure of any other item. Not dependent.
Failure mechanism	The physical, chemical, electrical, thermal, or other process which results in failure.
Failure mode	The consequence of the mechanism through which the failure occurs, i.e., short, open, fracture, excessive wear.
Failure, random	Failure whose occurrence is predictable only in a probabilistic or statistical sense. This applies to all distributions.
Failure rate	The total number of failures within an item population, divided by the total number of life units expended by that population, during a particular measurement interval under stated conditions.
Inherent R and M value	A measure of reliability or maintainability that includes only the effects of an item design and its application, and assumes an ideal operation and support environment.
Inventory, active	The group of items assigned an operational status.
Inventory, inactive	The group of items being held in reserve for possible future assignments to an operational status.
Item	A nonspecific term used to denote any product, including systems, materials, parts, subassemblies, sets, accessories, etc. (Source: MIL-STD-280)
Life units	A measure of duration applicable to the item, e.g., operating hours, cycles, distance, rounds fired, attempts to operate.

Maintainability	The measure of the ability of an item to be retained or restored to specified condition when maintenance is performed by personnel having specified skill levels, using prescribed procedures and resources, at each prescribed level of maintenance and repair.
Maintenance	All actions necessary for retaining an item in or restoring it to a specified condition.
Maintenance action rate	The reciprocal of the mean time between maintenance actions = 1/MTBMA
Maintenance, corrective	All actions performed, as a result of failure, to restore an item to a specified condition. Corrective maintenance can include any or all of the following steps: localization, isolation, disassembly, interchange, reassembly, alignment, and checkout.
Maintenance, preventive	All actions performed in an attempt to retain an item in a specified condition by providing systematic inspection, detection, and prevention of incipient failures.
Maintenance time constraint (t)	The maintenance time that is usually prescribed as a requirement of the mission.
Mean maintenance downtime (MDT)	Includes supply time, logistics time, administrative delays, active maintenance time, etc.
Mean-maintenance-time	The measure of item maintainability taking into account maintenance policy. The sum of preventive and corrective maintenance times, divided by the sum of scheduled and unscheduled maintenance events, during a stated period of time.
Mean-time-between-failure (MTBF)	A basic measure of reliability for repairable items: The mean number of life units during which all parts of the item perform within their specified limits, during a particular measurement interval under stated conditions.
Mean-time-between-maintenance (MTBM)	A measure of the reliability taking into account maintenance policy. The total number of life units expended by a given time, divided by the total number of maintenance events (scheduled and unscheduled) due to that item.
Mean-time-between-maintenance actions (MTBMA)	A measure of the system reliability parameter related to demand for maintenance manpower: The total number of system life units, divided by the total number of maintenance actions (preventive and corrective) during a stated period of time.
Mean-time-to-failure (MTTF)	A basic measure of system reliability for nonrepairable items: The total number of life units of an item divided by the total number of failures within that population, during a particular measurement interval under stated conditions.

Mean-time-to-repair (MTTR)	A basic measure of maintainability: The sum of corrective maintenance times at any specific level of repair, divided by the total number of failures within an item repaired at that level, during a particular interval under stated conditions.
Mission profile	A time-phased description of the events and environments an item experiences from initiation to completion of a specified mission, to include the criteria of mission success of critical failures.
Operable	The state of being able to perform the intended function.
Predicted	That which is expected at some future date, postulated on analysis of past experience and tests.
Redundancy	The existence of more than one means for accomplishing a given function. Each means of accomplishing the function need not necessarily be identical.
Redundancy, active	That redundancy wherein all redundant items are operating simultaneously.
Redundancy, standby	That redundancy wherein an alternative means of performing the function is not operating until it is activated upon failure of the primary means of performing the function.
Reliability	(1) The duration or probability of failure-free performance under stated conditions.
	(2) The probability that an item can perform its intended function for a specified interval under stated conditions. For nonredundant items this is equivalent to definition (1). For redundant items this is equivalent to definition of mission reliability.
Reliability, mission	The ability of an item to perform its required functions for the duration of a specified *mission profile.*
Repair	See *Maintenance, corrective*
Servicing	The performance of any act to keep an item in operating condition (i.e., lubrication, fueling, oiling, cleaning, etc.), but not including other preventive maintenance of parts or corrective maintenance.
Storage life	The length of time an item can be stored under specified conditions and still meet specified requirements.
Subsystem	A combination of sets, groups, etc. which performs an operational function within a system and is a major subdivision of the system, e.g., data processing subsystem, guidance subsystem.

System   General — A composite of equipment and skills, and techniques capable of performing or supporting an operational role, or both. A complete system includes all equipment, related facilities, material, software, services, and personnel required for its operation and support to the degree that it can be considered self-sufficient in its intended operational environment.

Time, active   That time during which an item is in an operational inventory.

Time, administrative   That element of *delay time* that is not included in *supply delay time*.

Time, alert   That element of uptime during which an item is assumed to be in specified operating condition and is awaiting a command to perform its intended mission.

Time, checkout   That element of *maintenance time* during which performance of an item is verified to be a specified condition.

Time, delay   That element of downtime during which no maintenance is being accomplished on the item because of either supply or administrative delay.

Time, down (downtime)   That element of active time during which an item is not in condition to perform its required function. (Reduces *availability* and *dependability*.)

Time, supply delay   That element of *delay time* during which a needed replacement item is being obtained.

Time, up (uptime)   That element of *active time* during which an item is in condition to perform its required functions. (Increases *availability and dependability*.)

Useful life   The number of life units from manufacture to when an item has an unrepairable failure or unacceptable failure rate.

Wearout   The process which results in an increase of the *failure rate* or probability of failure with increasing number of *life units*.

SYSTEM EFFECTIVENESS ▌▌

System effectiveness is the result of a combination of availability, dependability, and capability. The definition of *system effectiveness* is: A measure of the degree to which an item or system can be expected to achieve a set of specific mission requirements, and which may be expressed as a function of availability, dependability, and capability.

Availability   A measure of the degree to which an item or system is in the operable and commitable state at the start of the mission, when the mission is called for at an unknown point in time. The point in time is a random variable.

Where: F_C = Number of corrective actions per 1000 hr

F_P = Number of preventive actions per 1000 hr

$\overline{M}_{CT}$ = Mean-Active-Corrective-Maintenance-Time (MTTR)

$\overline{M}_{PT}$ = Mean-Active-Preventive-Maintenance-Time (scheduled downtime)

Example: MTBMA = 1200 hr, F_C = 1.0, F_P = 1.0, $\overline{M}_{CT}$ = 8.5, $\overline{M}_{PT}$ = 1.0

$$MMT = \frac{(1.0)\ (8.5)\ +\ (1.0)\ (1.0)}{1.0\ +\ 1.0} = 4.75$$

$$A_A = \frac{1200}{1200+4.75} = 0.9961 \text{ or } 99.61\%$$

3. Operational availability (A_O) = MTBMA/(MTBMA+MDT)

Example: MTBMA = 1200 hr
MDT = 8 hr

$$A_O = 1200/(1200+8) = 0.9934 \text{ or } 99.34\%$$

Operational availability is strongly affected by the ability to plan for corrective action, and to respond to system faults as quickly as possible when they occur.

3.0 RELIABILITY BATHTUB CURVE

Over the life of a complex system, three distinct failure rate phases may become apparent. The first phase or period is referred to as the *infant mortality* period, which is shown as the decreasing failure rate on the left portion of Figure 3.1. The second phase is the *random or constant cause* failure period, which is the period of time encompassing the flat portion of the curve, where the failure rate remains constant. The last phase is the *wearout period*, which is shown on the right side of Figure 3.1 as an increasing failure rate. The wearout phase is more predominant in mechanical systems than in electronic systems.

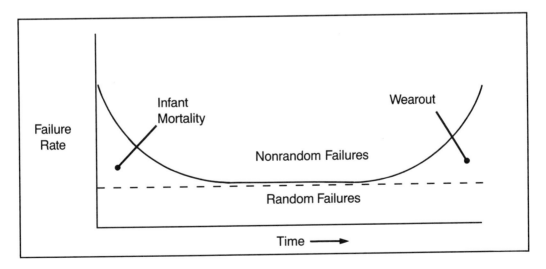

Figure 3.1 Reliability bathtub curve showing the *infant mortality* period as the decreasing failure rate (left), *random constant cause* failure period (middle), and *wearout period* as an increasing failure rate (right).

Infant mortality failures are generally the result of manufacturing errors that are not caught in inspection prior to burn-in or placing in service. Failures resulting from time/stress dependent errors may occur in this period.

Random failures and *wearout failures* are generally a factor of design.

No distinct break off from infant mortality to random to wearout failure has been established. Random failures can occur anywhere in the three periods, as can infant mortality failures. A failure caused by a cold solder joint may occur well into the service life, but this is really an infant mortality type failure. Wearout of mechanical parts also begins the moment the product is put into service.

The probability distributions occurring most often during the infant mortality period are Weibull, gamma, and decreasing exponential. Probability distributions of value in the constant failure rate period are exponential and Weibull. During the wearout period, the curves generally follow the normal or Weibull distributions.

Figure 3.2 is the same as shown in Figure 3.1, except that the nonrandom failure period has been designated as the constant failure rate period.

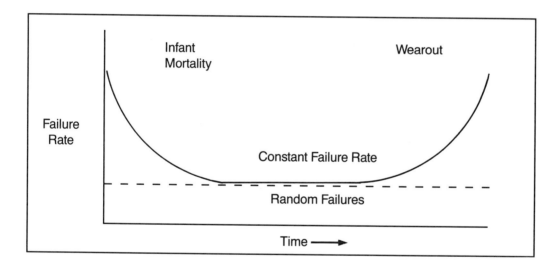

Figure 3.2 Reliability bathtub curve showing nonrandom failure period as the constant failure rate period.

DOCUMENTS RELATING TO RELIABILITY REQUIREMENTS ▌▌▌▌▌▌▌▌▌▌▌▌▌▌▌▌▌▌▌

The following is a list of standards used in reliability work:

MIL-STD-415   Test provision for electronic systems and associated equipment

MIL-STD-446   Environmental requirements for electric parts

MIL-STD-470   Maintainability program requirements for system and equipment

MIL-STD-471   Maintainability demonstration

MIL-STD-690   Failure rate sampling plans and procedures

MIL-STD-721   Definitions of effectiveness terms for reliability, maintainability. Human factors and safety

MIL-STD-756   Reliability prediction

MIL-STD-757   Reliability evaluation from demonstration data

MIL-STD-781   Reliability design qualification and production acceptance tests: exponential distribution

MIL-STD-785   Reliability program for systems and equipment — development and production

MIL-STD-810   Environmental test methods

TECHNICAL REPORTS   Sampling procedures and tables for life testing based on the Weibull distribution. OASD installation and logistics, Washington

                           — TR 3 Mean life criterion
                           — TR 4 Hazard rate criterion
                           — TR 6 Reliable life criterion

MIL-STD 1556   Government/industry data exchange program contractor participation requirements

MIL-HDBK 108   Sampling procedures and tables for life and reliability test

MIL-HDBK 109   Statistical procedures for determining validity of suppliers attributed inspection

MIL-HDBK 217   Reliability prediction of electronic equipment

RELIABILITY TEXTBOOKS ▌▌

A listing of texts that should be of interest to those pursuing further studies in the reliability and maintainability engineering fields is shown in the bibliography.

4.0 EXPONENTIAL DISTRIBUTION

The exponential distribution (Figure 4.1) is the most commonly used distribution in reliability, and is generally used to predict the probability of survival to time (t).

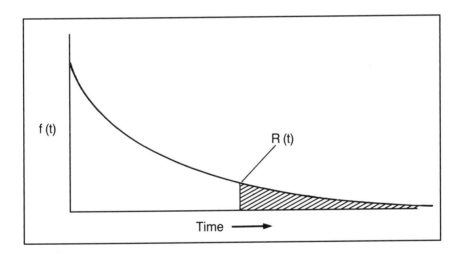

Figure 4.1   The exponential distribution is the most commonly used distribution in reliability.

The probability density function (pdf) of the exponential is:

$$f(t) = \lambda e^{-\lambda t} \quad \text{or}$$

$$f(t) = \frac{1}{\Theta} e^{-t/\Theta} \quad \text{where } t \geq 0$$

MTBF = Θ

λ = failure rate = $1/\Theta$

R (t) = $e^{-\lambda t}$ or $e^{-t/\Theta}$, where t $\geq$ 0

F (t) = Unreliability = $1 - R(t)$

The hazard function for the exponential distribution = λ, and is constant throughout the function. Therefore, the exponential distribution should only be used for reliability prediction during the constant failure rate or chance cause failure period of operation.

Some unique features to the exponential distribution include:

1. The mean and standard deviation are equal.

2. Of all the values 63.21% fall below the mean value, which translates into only a 36.79% chance of surviving past the time period of one MTBF.

3. Reliability as time t approaches zero, approaches one as a limit.

As discussed earlier, the reliability for a given time (t) during the constant failure rate period can be calculated with the formula:

$$R_{(t)} = e^{-\lambda t}$$

Where: e = base of the natural logarithms which is 2.718281828. . .

λ = failure rate
t = time

Example: The equipment in a packaging plant has a failure rate of 0.001/hr (MTBF = 1000 hr). What is the probability of operating for a period of 500 hr without failure?
λ = 0.001, t = 500
$e^{-\lambda t} = e^{-(0.001)(500)} = e^{-0.5} = 0.6065$

A 60.65% probability of operating for a period of 500 hr without failure exists when the MTBF = 1000 hr (λ = 0.001).

Note: MTBF and λ do not need to be a function of time in hours. The characteristic of "time" or usage can be such units as cycles rather than hours. In this case, the MCBF would be the appropriate measure.

Example: One cycle of the machine completes the assembly of 24 units. A study of this machine predicted an MCBF of 15,000 cycles (λ = 0.0000667/cycle).

What is the probability of operating 16,000 cycles without failure?

Note: λ is also a function of cycles.

The reliability for this example can be calculated from either equation noted earlier.

(1) $R_{(t)} = e^{-t/\Theta}$ or $e^{-c/\Theta}$; where c = cycles, or (2) $R_{(t)} = e^{-\lambda t}$ or $e^{-\lambda c}$

For this example equation 1 will be used.

$R_{(16,000)} = e^{-16,000/15,000} = e^{-1.0667} = 0.3442$

A 34.42% probability exists that the machine will run 16,000 cycles without failure.

An interesting note of prediction during the chance cause failure period is that the probability of functioning for a given time period (t) is totally independent of previous operation. Therefore, as long as operation remains in the chance cause failure mode, the probability of failure is the same during the first 100 hr of operation or for the period of 10,000 hr to 10,100 hr.

FUNDAMENTALS OF RELIABILITY STATISTICS ▮▮▮▮▮▮▮▮▮▮▮▮▮▮▮▮▮▮▮▮▮▮▮▮▮▮▮▮▮▮▮▮

Among the many reliability statistical applications, there are relatively few mathematical relationships that provide a large part of reliability calculations. Some of these include: hazard function, survival, series systems, parallel systems, perfect and imperfect switching for standby redundancy, confidence intervals for MTBF, and others.

Although the concepts of reliability theory will not be explored completely, the following definition of reliability will be used throughout:

Reliability: The probability that an item will perform its intended function for a specified interval understated environmental conditions.

When making predictions using the exponential distribution, it is imperative that the failure rate in this period be constant; failures are random in nature. This is also known as the chance cause or useful life period. Other periods of failure are early or infant mortality and wearout.

ESTIMATING MTBF

An important function of reliability prediction is the estimation of the mean life parameter Θ, generally referred to as the MTBF. The general equation for estimating MTBF is:

Equation R1: $\hat{\Theta} = T/r$

Where: T = total test time of all items for both failed and nonfailed items.

r = the total number of failures occurring during the test.

Example: The total test time on an actuator was 316 hr, and during this time four failures occurred. What is the estimate of the MTBF?

$\hat{\Theta} = 316/4 = 79$ hr.

6.0 CENSORING AND MTBF CALCULATIONS

At times several items are tested simultaneously and the results are combined to estimate the MTBF. When performing tests of this type, two common test situations occur.

The first is when a total of n items are placed on test. Each test stand operates each test item a given number of hours or cycles. As test items fail, they are replaced. The test time is defined in advance, so the test is said to be truncated after the specified number of hours or cycles. A time or cycle truncated test is called *type I censoring*. The formula for a type I censoring situation follows:

Equation R2: $\hat{\Theta} = n\tau/r$

Where: $\hat{\Theta}$ = estimate of MTBF or MCBF
  n = number of items on test
  τ = total test time or cycles per unit
  r = number of failures occurring during the test

This formula is similar to that shown in equation R1.

Example: 12 items were placed on test for a test time of 50,000 cycles each (a total of 600,000 cycles). As units failed they were repaired or replaced with new units. During the test, nine failures occurred. What is the estimate of the MCBF? (Remember that $\hat{\Theta}$ is the estimate of MCBF.)

$\hat{\Theta} = (12)\,(50{,}000)/9 = 66{,}666.67$

The estimate of the MCBF is 66,666.67 cycles.

The second test situation is the case where n items are placed on test at one time, and the test is to be truncated (stopped) after a total of r failures occurs. As items fail, they are not replaced or repaired and are placed back on test. A failure truncated test design is referred to as *type II censoring*.

The formula for estimating $\hat{\Theta}$ in a type II censoring test design is given as:

$$\textit{Equation R3: } \hat{\Theta} = \frac{\sum_{i=1}^{r} y_i + (n-r) y_r}{r}$$

Where: $\hat{\Theta}$ = estimate of MCBF or MTBF
y_i = time to failure of the i_{th} item
y_r = time to failure of the unit at which time the test is truncated

Example: A total of 20 items are placed on test. The test is to be truncated when the fourth failure occurs. The failures occur at the following number of hours into the test.

Failure No.	Test Hr
1	$y_1 =$ 317
2	$y_2 =$ 736
3	$y_3 =$ 1032
4	$y_4 =$ 1335
r = 4	$\Sigma y_i =$ 3420

The remaining 16 items were in good operating order when the test was truncated at the fourth failure.

Using equation R3, the result is:

$$\hat{\Theta} = \frac{3420 + 16\,(1335)}{4} = 6195$$

The estimate of the MTBF = 6195 hr.

RELIABILITY PREDICTION

The most common and fortunately simplest calculation for reliability of an item during the constant failure rate period is:

Equation R4: $R_{(t)} = e^{-\lambda t}$

Where: $R_{(t)}$ is the reliability for a period of time (t).
   e is the base of the natural logarithms (2.718281828).
   t is the time period under consideration.
   λ is the failure rate or the reciprocal of MTBF.
   MTBF is the mean-time-between-failures.

Example: An item fails on the average of once every 10,000 hours (MTBF = 10,000 hr). What is the probability of survival for 2000 hr?

Using the above formula, $\lambda = 1/10,000 = 0.0001/\text{hr}$. $R_{(2000)} = e^{-(0.0001)(2000)} = e^{-0.2} = 0.8187$

The probability of survival for 2000 hr is 0.8187 or 81.87%. The probability of survival for 10,000 hr $= e^{-1} = 0.3679$. There is greater than a 63% chance of failure at an item's or system's MTBF.

8.0 CONFIDENCE INTERVALS FOR MTBF

The calculation of the MTBF (Θ) is, like $\overline{X}$ and s, a point estimate. An improvement in this estimate in the form of a confidence interval is required in some cases. Confidence intervals allow a band or interval to be put around the point estimate which adds more meaning to the estimate. For example, a 90% confidence interval means that 90% of the intervals calculated in this manner from sample data will contain the true (but unknown) mean, while 10% will not. At 95% confidence, 95% of the intervals calculated will contain the true mean while 5% will not. The higher the level of confidence, the wider will be the confidence interval. When assuming an exponential distribution (constant failure rate) the chi-square distribution can be used to calculate these confidence intervals.

In reliability testing to estimate MTBF (Θ) two situations exist. The first is testing for a given period of time (type I censoring); the second case is testing to a predetermined number of failures (type II censoring). While the differences are in testing design, there is also a difference in the calculation of the lower confidence limit based on the test method used.

8.1 TESTING TO A PREDETERMINED NUMBER OF FAILURES

When testing to a predetermined number of failures, the following equations are used:
Lower one-sided confidence limit —

Equation R5: $\dfrac{2T}{\chi^2_{(\alpha,\,2r)}} \leq \Theta$

Where: T = test time
α = level of risk (1 − confidence)
r = number of failures

Two-sided confidence interval —

Equation R6:

$$LCL = \frac{2T}{\chi^2_{(\alpha/2, \, 2r)}}$$

$$UCL = \frac{2T}{\chi^2_{(1-\alpha/2, \, 2r)}}$$

UCL = upper confidence limit
LCL = lower confidence limit

$$LCL \leq \Theta \leq UCL$$

Example: A unit is tested until the fourth failure. Total test time when the fourth failure occurs is 5000 hr. Calculate the one-sided lower confidence interval at 90% confidence ($\alpha = .10$); calculate the two-sided confidence interval at 90% confidence ($\alpha = 0.10$, $\alpha/2 = 0.05$, $1 - \alpha/2 = 0.95$).

One-sided interval —

$$\frac{2 \, (5000)}{13.362} \leq \Theta$$

Note: 13.362 is χ^2 value for $\alpha = 0.10$ and $2r = 8$ degrees of freedom (df).

$$\frac{10,000}{13.362} \leq \Theta$$

$$748.39 \leq \Theta \text{ with } 90\% \text{ confidence}$$

While the point estimate for Θ is 5000/4 which is 1250 hr, the 90% one-sided lower confidence limit is 748.39 hr.

Two-sided interval —

$$\frac{2 \, (5000)}{15.507} \leq \Theta \leq \frac{2 \, (5000)}{2.733}$$

Where: 2.733 is χ^2 value for $1 - \alpha/2$ and 8 df
15.507 is χ^2 value for $\alpha/2$ and 8 df
$644.87 \leq \Theta \leq 3658.98$

8.2 TESTING FOR A PREDETERMINED TIME ∎∎∎∎∎∎∎∎∎∎∎

When testing for a predetermined time, the following equations are used:

Lower one-sided confidence limit —

Equation R7: $\dfrac{2T}{\chi^2_{(\alpha,\,2r+2)}} \leq \Theta$

Note: That the df for χ^2 is 2r+2.

Two-sided confidence interval —

Equation R8:

$$LCL = \dfrac{2T}{\chi^2_{(\alpha/2,\,2r+2)}}$$

$$UCL = \dfrac{2T}{\chi^2_{(1-\alpha/2,\,2r)}}$$

$$LCL \leq \Theta \leq UCL$$

UCL = upper confidence limit
LCL = lower confidence limit

Note: The lower limit uses 2r+2 df while the upper limit uses 2r df. This allows for a lower estimate of the MTBF even if no failures have occurred, although no estimate can be given of the upper limit without failures occurring during testing when using these equations.

Example: A unit is tested for a total of 3000 hr. When testing was stopped after 3000 hr, it was noted that three failures had occurred during testing. Calculate at 90% confidence both the one-sided lower limit and two-sided confidence interval for the MTBF (Θ).

$$\text{Point estimate } \Theta = \dfrac{3000 \text{ hr}}{3} = 1000 \text{ hr}$$

One-sided limit —

$$\dfrac{2\,(3000)}{13.362} \leq \Theta$$

$449.03 \leq \Theta$, with 90% confidence.

Two-sided interval —

$$\dfrac{2\,(3000)}{15.507} \leq \Theta \leq \dfrac{2\,(3000)}{1.635}$$

$$386.9 \leq \Theta \leq 3669.7$$

The 90% confidence interval is from 386.9 to 3669.7 hr.

Note: In most cases the lower confidence limit is the only one of interest.

8.3 FAILURE-FREE TESTING ■■■■■■■■■■■■■■■■■■■■■■■■■■■■■■■■■■■

When no failures are allowed or occur in a test for a predetermined amount of time the one-sided lower limit calculation is simplified to:

Equation R9: $\quad - \dfrac{nT}{\ln\alpha} \leq MTBF$

Where: T is test time
   n = sample size
   α = level of significance

Example: Fifty units are tested without failure for 100 hr. What is the 95% lower confidence limit for the MTBF? Using equation R9:

$$- \frac{(50)\,(100)}{\ln(0.05)} \leq MTBF$$

$$1669.04 \text{ hr} \leq MTBF$$

9.0 SYSTEM RELIABILITY

9.1 SERIES SYSTEMS

In many cases there are several, hundreds, or thousands of components to a system. This occurs often, and the failure of one component in the system may result in total system failure. This is quite apparent in computer systems.

When the system is comprised of many components, and the failure of one results in system failure, this is called a *series system*. The reliability of a series system is a product of the component subsystem reliabilities.

Example: The system shown in Figure 9.1 contains three components in series with reliabilities of 0.95, 0.90, and 0.80. What is the system reliability?

$$R_{(s)} = 0.95 \times 0.90 \times 0.80 = 0.684 \text{ or } 68.4\%$$

More often the individual failure rates for the system components are given along with the system life requirements in time or cycles. When these characteristics are known, the reliability of the system can be expressed by the following equation:

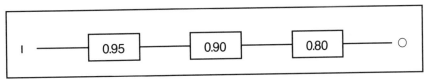

Figure 9.1   Three components in series with reliabilities of 0.95, 0.90, and 0.80.

Equation R10: $R_{s(t)} = e^{-\Sigma\lambda_i t_i}$
                        i = 1 through N.

N = the total number of components in the system.

Where: $\Sigma\lambda_i t_i$ = the sum of the individual failure rates multiplied by the time active. In most cases the time is the same for all components, reducing the equation to: $t\Sigma\lambda_i$

Example: The three components in series shown in Figure 9.2 have the following failure rates per hour: component 1 = 0.0001/hr; component 2 = 0.00005/hr; and component 3 = 0.00001/hr. What is the probability of survival for 100 hr?

Failure rates are additive.

$\Sigma\lambda_i = 0.0001 + 0.00005 + 0.00001 = 0.00016$
$\Sigma\lambda_i = 0.00016$
$\Sigma\lambda_i t = (0.00016)\,(100) = 0.016$
$R_s(100) = e^{-0.016} = 0.9841$ or 98.41%

Note how extremely low failure rates (high MTBFs) result in a low probability of survival for a relatively short period of time when placed in series. Here the MTBFs are 10,000 hr, 20,000 hr, and 100,000 hr; yet in series they only have about 98.5% probability of surviving 100 hr.

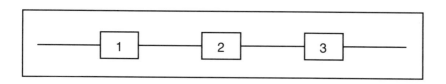

Figure 9.2   Three components in series with failure rates of 0.0001/hr, 0.00005/hr, and 0.00001/hr.

9.2 PARALLEL SYSTEMS ▌▌▌▌▌▌▌▌▌▌▌▌▌▌▌▌▌▌▌▌▌▌▌▌▌▌▌▌▌▌

Series systems do not offer a high level of confidence in high risk situations. This is especially felt when the risk is to oneself. Therefore, the goal is to increase confidence and lower risk of injury or death at the same time. One method of attaining this goal is redundancy. Two types of redundancy will be covered in more detail later: active and standby. While redundancy affords higher confidence in the probability of success for the mission at hand, it also has a penalty of increased cost, weight, package size, maintenance, etc. The key here is in trade-offs. While trade-offs may not appear to be ethical where human life is concerned, they seem to be necessary. For example, to satisfy everyone's concern for safety on a space launch the redundancy would result in a craft so heavy it would not be able to leave the ground. Safe? Yes! Mission accomplished? No!

9.2.1 ACTIVE PARALLEL SYSTEMS ||||||||||||||||||||||||||||||||

The most common form of redundancy is active parallel redundancy. Active means that both components are active or functioning during the life of the system. A scheme of an active parallel system is shown in Figure 9.3.

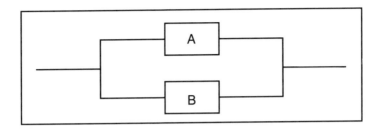

Figure 9.3 Schema of an active parallel system.

Components A and B are both active. When the system is active, if both A and B are functioning, the system will operate. If A fails and B survives, the system will operate. If A survives and B fails, the system will operate. When A and B both fail, system failure occurs. When several components are in parallel and have equal failure rates, the result is a binomial distribution calculation.

Example: In the previous diagram, the reliability of component A is 0.99 and the reliability of B is 0.95. What is the reliability of the parallel redundant system? To calculate the reliability of the redundant system, the following formula is used:

Equation R11: $R(s) = R_1 + R_2 - R_1 R_2$
$R(s) = 0.99 + 0.95 - (0.99)(0.95) = 0.9995$

If both components have equal failure rates, the equation becomes:

Equation R12: $R_{(s)} = 2R - R^2$

Example: In the diagram shown in Figure 9.4, components C and D have reliabilities of 0.99 each. What is the reliability for the parallel system?

$$R_{(s)} = 2(0.99) - (0.99)^2 = 0.9999$$

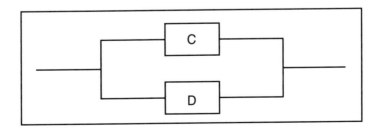

Figure 9.4 Components C and D have reliabilities of 0.99 each.

In most cases, the individual reliabilities of the components are not known per se, but values are given for failure rates and time. Rather than convert these values into probabilities and then solve, the given values may be used directly.

In this case equation R11 becomes:

Equation R13: $R_{(t)} = e^{-\lambda_1 t} + e^{-\lambda_2 t} - e^{-(\lambda_1 + \lambda_2)t}$

Equation R14: $R_{(t)} = 2e^{-\lambda t} - e^{-2\lambda t}$

9.2.2 BINOMIAL DISTRIBUTION ■■■■■■■■■■■■■■■■■■■■■■■■■■■■■■■■■■■■■

When several components are in parallel with equal failure rates and any one of the components will carry the system load, this can be resolved into a cumulative binomial distribution calculation. For example, if three components are in parallel and only one is required for system success, the system will operate when there are zero failures, one failure, or two failures. The system will function until the third failure occurs, or, in other words, when two or less failures have occurred in three trials.

Example: Three units are in parallel. The system units all have a known reliability of 0.99. If one unit is sufficient to carry the load, what is the reliability of the parallel system? Using the binomial distribution, the result is:

$$P_{(0)} = C^3_0 \, (.99)^3(.01)^0 = 0.970299$$

$$P_{(1)} = C^3_1 \, (.99)^2(.01)^1 = 0.029403$$

$$P_{(2)} = C^3_2 \, (.99)^1(.01)^2 = 0.000297$$

$$\text{Total} = 0.999999$$

The probability of two or less failures or system reliability for this configuration is 0.999999. At this time, it is prudent to remind the reader that the number of significant digits in the final answer cannot exceed the number of significant digits supplied in the problem.

When calculating equations for three components in parallel when all are not equal the following equation is used:

Equation R15: $R_{(s)} = R_1 + R_2 + R_3 - R_1 R_2 - R_2 R_3 - R_1 R_3 + R_1 R_2 R_3$

If all components are equal, then use the following equation:

Equation R16: $R_{(s)} = 3R - 3R^2 + R^3$

9.3 STANDBY PARALLEL SYSTEMS ▐▐▐▐▐▐▐▐▐▐▐▐▐▐▐▐▐▐▐▐▐

Further reliability improvement can be achieved on redundant systems by the addition of a switch between components. In these systems, the unit on standby is usually considered dormant with zero probability of failure. Although additional gains are made in survival probability, remember the penalties of weight, size, cost, etc.

9.3.1 EQUAL FAILURE RATES — PERFECT SWITCHING ▐▐▐▐▐▐▐▐▐▐

The case of equal failure rates and perfect switching is the most basic version in this series. The formula for this design is:

Equation R17: $R_{(t)} = e^{-\lambda t} + \lambda t e^{-\lambda t}$

Equation R18: $R_{(t)} = e^{-\lambda t} (1+\lambda t)$

Example: Two identical components are used in a redundant design. One unit is active and the other unit is standing by to be placed in service if the first unit fails. The failure rate for each component is 0.001/hr and the switching is considered perfect. What is the 500 hr reliability for this system?

Using equation R18 the result is:

$e^{-(.001)\,(500)} (1+(.001)\,(500))$

$e^{-0.5} (1.5) = 0.9098$

The probability of survival for 500 hr is 0.9098. If this was simple active redundancy (no switch), the $P_{(s)}$ would be 0.8452; thus, an improvement of 7.6% was made by the addition of the switch.

For n items in a standby configuration (of which the previous two-item case is a derivation), the reliability of the system can be calculated by the following equation:

Equation R19: $R_s^n(t) = (e^{-\lambda t}) \sum_{i=0}^{n} (\lambda t)^i / i!$

While this equation was generalized, the equations that are shown in sections 9.3.2, 9.3.3, 9.3.4, and 9.4 cannot be so easily reduced into one basic general equation.

9.3.2 UNEQUAL FAILURE RATES — PERFECT SWITCHING ▐▐▐▐▐▐▐

In many cases, the two units are not identical such as with a generator that has a battery backup. Again, no failure rate for the battery in its standby mode is assumed. The equation for this design is:

Equation R20: $R_{(t)} = e^{-\lambda_1 t} + \dfrac{\lambda_1}{\lambda_2 - \lambda_1} (e^{-\lambda_1 t} - e^{-\lambda_2 t})$

Example: A power generator has a failure rate of 0.001/hr. On standby, in case of generator failure, is a battery pack with a failure rate of 0.005/hr. If perfect switching is assumed, what is the system reliability for one week (168 hr)?

Using equation R20, the result is:

$$R_{(168)} = e^{-(.001)\,(168)} + \frac{.001}{.005 - .001}\{e^{-(.001)\,(168)} - e^{-(.005)\,(168)}\}$$

$$R_{(168)} = 0.9488$$

Note: The reliability of a simple parallel redundant system (no switch, both units active for time t) has a reliability of 0.9121. Thus, with the addition of a switch an improvement of 4.13 % was achieved.

9.3.3 EQUAL FAILURE RATES — IMPERFECT SWITCHING ▮▮▮▮▮▮

There are cases where the switch to a backup device is done on a remote basis automatically with less than perfect reliability. In this instance, the switch reliability must be taken into account. The formula for this design is:

Equation R21: $R_{(t)} = e^{-\lambda t}\{1 + R(sw)\,\lambda t\}$

Example: Two units as shown in Figure 9.5 are in parallel (standby configuration) with a switch that has a reliability of 0.95 per operation. The failure rates of the components in parallel are 0.0005/hr. What is the reliability of this configuration for 100 hr? See Figure 9.5 for a schematic view.

Using equation R21 the result is:

$$e^{-(.0005)\,(100)}\{1 + 0.95(0.0005\,(100)\} = 0.9964$$

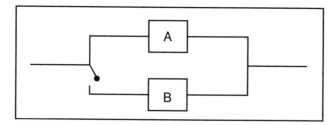

Figure 9.5 Two units are in parallel standby configuration with a reliability of 0.95 per operation.

9.3.4 UNEQUAL FAILURE RATES — IMPERFECT SWITCHING ▮▮▮▮

As in the previous section switching is considered imperfect. The difference, though, is in the backup unit which may be different from the primary unit with the accompanying difference in failure rate. The formula for this design is:

Equation R22:

$$R_{(t)} = e^{-\lambda_1 t} + R_{(sw)} \frac{\lambda_1}{\lambda_2 - \lambda_1} [e^{-\lambda_1 t} - e^{-\lambda_2 t}]$$

Example: (Use diagram from previous section.) Two units as shown in Figure 9.5 are in parallel (standby) with a switch that has a reliability of 0.99 per operation. The failure rate of component A is 0.0001/hr and component B is 0.001/hr. What is the reliability of this configuration for 100 hr?

Using equation R22, the result is:

$$R_{(100)} =$$

$$e^{-(.0001)(100)} + 0.99 \frac{0.0001}{.001 - .0001} [e^{-(.0001)(100)} - e^{-(.001)(100)}]$$

$$R_{(100)} = 0.9994$$

9.4 SHARED LOAD PARALLEL SYSTEMS ▮▮▮▮▮▮▮▮▮▮▮▮▮▮▮

Shared load parallel systems are active parallel systems where the units in parallel are identical. The difference between this and the simple parallel system is that the failure rate for the surviving component increases upon failure of the first component. Proponents of this design claim this approach is intuitively more realistic than the simple active parallel design. They propose that loading increases in the surviving component are a natural result of first component failure. The formula for this design is (exponential distribution assumed):

Equation R23:

$$R_{(t)} = e^{-2\lambda_1 t} + \frac{2\lambda_1}{(2\lambda_1 - \lambda_2)} (e^{-\lambda_2 t} - e^{-2\lambda_1 t})$$

Where: $\lambda_1 t$ is the failure rate when both components are in the operable condition.

$\lambda_2 t$ is the failure rate of the surviving component when one component has failed.

Example: A power plant is served by two cooling systems in parallel. Operational data have shown that one system will properly cool the plant but the additional stress on the cooling system results in a higher failure rate. The failure rate of the single cooling system (λ_2) is 0.001 per hr. When the cooling systems are working in parallel or with shared load the failure rate per unit is 0.0001 per hr. What is the 24 hr reliability of this system?

Using equation R23, the result is:

$R_{(24)} =$

$$e^{-2\,(.0001)\,(24)} + \frac{2\,(.0001)}{[2\,(.0001) - .001]}\,(e^{-(.001)\,(24)} - e^{-2\,(.0001)\,(24)})$$

$R_{(24)} = 0.995212 + (-0.25)\,(0.976286 - 0.995212) = 0.999943$

The reliability for this configuration for a 24 hr period is greater than 99.99%.

10.0 BAYES' THEOREM APPLICATION

Sometimes a reliability diagram cannot be reduced easily to a basic series or parallel structure. An example of this is shown in Figure 10.1. The system will operate properly if either AE or parallel systems BD operate, but component C has been added to enhance the reliability of the system, and the system is not a simple parallel system. The system can operate with inputs to A, B, or C.

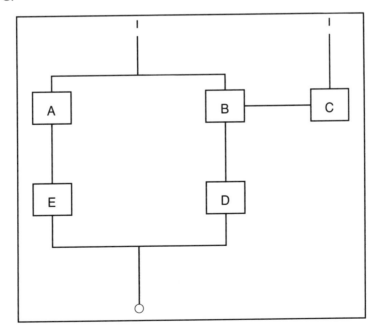

Figure 10.1 Reliability diagram that cannot be reduced easily to a basic series or parallel structure.

The use of Bayes' theorem requires the identification of what is termed a *keynote component*. This keynote component can be identified as a component that enhances reliability of the system by its addition, but still lets the system operate if it fails. This component is a form of partial redundancy.

Bayes' theorem can be worded as follows:

The probability of system failure is the probability that the system fails given that the keynote component is good, multiplied by the probability that the keynote component is good, *plus* the probability that the system fails if the keynote component is bad, multiplied by the probability that the keynote component is bad.

If the keynote component is identified as (C), the probability of system failure is:

$P_{(F)}$ = {P (system failure if C is good) × P (C is good) + P (system failure if C is bad) × P (C is bad)}

The equation is not as formidable to apply as it reads, as is shown by the following example.

Example: Using the diagram shown in Figure 10.2 and failure rates listed, calculate the probability of system failure during 10 hours of operation.

In Figure 10.2 the following failure rates apply: Component A = 0.005/hr, Component B = 0.005/hr, Component C = 0.004/hr, Component D = 0.006/hr, and Component E = 0.007/hr.

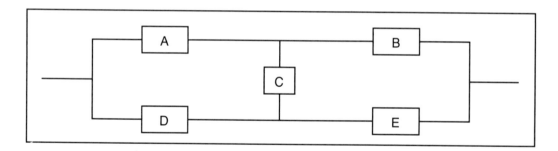

Figure 10.2   Series Parallel system with component C added to enhance reliability.

Solution

Bayes' probability theorem for the occurrence of F is given by:

P (F) = P (F, given B_i) P (B_i) + P (F, given B_j) P (B_j)

This can be rewritten in terms of this problem as:
P (system failure if component C is good) × P (C is good) + P (system failure if C is bad) × P (C is bad)

In this problem, component C would be defined as the keynote component. If component C is considered to be good, Figure 10.2 reduces to the diagram shown in Figure 10.3.

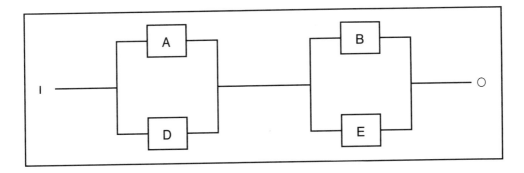

Figure 10.3 Diagram that results if component C in Figure 10.2 is good.

The reliability for component A for 10 hr = 0.95122
The reliability for component B for 10 hr = 0.95122
The reliability for component C for 10 hr = 0.96078
The reliability for component D for 10 hr = 0.94176
The reliability for component E for 10 hr = 0.93239

The reliability for the configuration in Figure 10.3 = 0.99387

Unreliability = 1 − 0.993871995 = 0.00613

Step 1 = P $_{\text{(Failure if C is good)}}$ P $_{\text{(C is good)}}$
= (0.00613) × (0.960789) = 0.00589

Thus, the first half of the required term shown as step 1 equals 0.00589.

If component C is considered *bad*, Figure 10.2 reduces to the diagram shown in Figure 10.4.

The reliability for the configuration in Figure 10.4 = 0.9884.

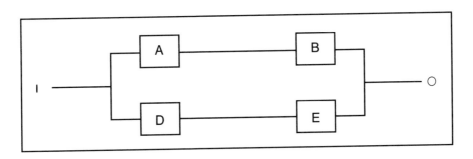

Figure 10.4 Diagram that results if component C in Figure 10.2 is bad.

Unreliability = 1 − 0.9884 = 0.0116

Step 2 = P $_{\text{(Failure if C is bad)}}$ P $_{\text{(C is bad)}}$

= (0.0116) × (0.0392) = 0.000455

Thus, the second half of the required term shown as step 2 equals 0.000455

Total unreliability = the sum of steps 1 and 2 = 0.00589 + 0.000455
Total unreliability = **0.00634**

BETA DISTRIBUTION

The beta distribution is used to determine a lower confidence limit for the fraction nonconforming (p) at a predetermined confidence level (γ). The beta distribution is dual to the binomial distribution which allows the lower confidence limit to be determined as a percentage point on the beta distribution.

The confidence limits (γ) given in Table A include: 0.5, 0.75, 0.9, 0.95, 0.99, and 0.995.

Example 1: A sample of 50 units is tested with two failures noted. Determine the lower limit for reliability at $\gamma = 0.95$ (95% confidence).

Where: n = sample size = 50
       s = number of successes = 48
       r = number of failures = 2

In Table A, the value for $\gamma = 0.95$ for n = 50, s = 48, and r = 2, is 0.882. Therefore, the 95% lower confidence limit for reliability is 0.882 or 88.2%.

Example 2: A sample of 10 units is tested with one failure noted. Determine the lower limit for reliability at 90% confidence.
       n = 10, s = 9, r = 1, $\gamma = 0.90$

The table value (Table A) for this combination is 0.690. Therefore, the 90% lower confidence limit on reliability is 69%.

12.0 NONPARAMETRIC AND RELATED TEST DESIGNS

12.1 CALCULATING RELIABILITY IN ZERO FAILURES SITUATIONS ▮▮▮▮▮▮▮▮▮▮▮▮▮▮▮▮▮▮▮▮▮▮▮▮▮▮▮▮▮▮▮▮▮▮▮▮▮▮

When calculating the lower confidence limit for reliability when no failures are to be allowed during testing the situation is simplified by the use of the following equation.

Equation R24: $R_L = \alpha^{1/n}$

Where: R_L = the lower limit of reliability at level of significance desired
$\quad\quad\; \alpha$ = level of significance (1 − confidence)
$\quad\quad\; n$ = sample size

Example: Fifty units are tested without failure. What is the 95% confidence level of reliability?

Using equation R24: $R_L = (0.05)^{1/50}$
$\quad\quad\quad\quad\quad\quad\quad\; R_L = 0.9418$

Therefore, there is 95% confidence that the reliability is at least 94.18%.

12.2 SAMPLE SIZE DETERMINATION ▮▮▮▮▮▮▮▮▮▮▮▮▮▮▮▮▮▮▮▮▮▮▮

In the previous example, the sample size was given and the reliability level calculated. In many cases this will not suffice. The question could be stated: How large of a sample size must be tested without failure to demonstrate 95% confidence of 95% reliability. To calculate the required sample size use the following equation:

Equation R25: $n = \dfrac{\ln\,(1-\text{confidence})}{\ln\,\text{reliability}}$

Where: Confidence = confidence level desired
  (1 − confidence) = level of significance
  Reliability = demonstration level for reliability

Example: $n = \dfrac{\ln(1 - 0.95)}{\ln(0.95)} = \dfrac{-2.995732}{-0.051293} = 58.404$

This is rounded to 59 as 58 would only result in 95% confidence of 94.97%, which for all practical purposes may be acceptable, but it does not meet the specification required.

13.0 HAZARD FUNCTION

The hazard function is also known as the *instantaneous failure rate* and is the limit of the failure rate as the interval of time approaches zero ($\Delta \to 0$).

The hazard function can be expressed as the relationship between the probability density function (pdf) and the reliability function ($R_{(t)}$).

Basic relationships defining the hazard function are:

$$h_{(t)} = \text{hazard function} = f_{(t)}/R_{(t)}$$

$$R_{(t)} = \exp\left(-\int_{0}^{t} h(u)\, du\right)$$

$$f_{(t)} = h_{(t)} \exp\left(-\int_{0}^{t} h(u)\, du\right)$$

Example: A number of items (NI) are placed on test. The start of the test time $= 0$ ($t = 0$). $S =$ the number of items surviving at a given time (t). $P_{(st)} =$ the probability of survival (reliability) at time t.

The expected value for the number of items (a random variable) surviving at time t is given by:

$$E\{S_{(t)}\} = \overline{(NI)}\,(t) = (NI)\,R_{(t)}$$

$$R_{(t)} = \frac{\overline{(NI)}\,(t)}{(NI)}$$

$$F_{(t)} = 1 - R_{(t)}$$

$$f_{(t)} = \lim_{\Delta \to O} \frac{(\overline{NI})\,(t) - [(\overline{NI})\,(t + \Delta t)]}{(NI)\,\Delta t}$$

$$h_{(t)} = \lim_{\Delta \to O} \frac{(\overline{NI})\,(t) - [(\overline{NI})\,(t + \Delta t)]}{(NI)\,t\Delta t}$$

Therefore: $\dfrac{(NI)}{(NI)\,(t)} \quad f_{(t)} = f_{(t)}/R_{(t)}$

WEAROUT DISTRIBUTION

In mechanical reliability applications, wearout modes are important contributions to the failure patterns of complex equipment. The wearout life for common components can be determined by testing and/or by historical data. The standard deviation of wearout failures can be reasonably approximated by a sample of 30 to 50 pieces, and may be considered known, rather than estimated from sample data to simplify the calculation. If the standard deviation is not known, use the "One-Sided Statistical Tolerance Limit Factors 'K' for a Normal Distribution." This table can be found in Appendix II of *Juran's Quality Control Handbook* by Juran and Gryna (1988).

CASE 1 — STANDARD DEVIATION KNOWN ∎∎∎∎∎∎∎∎∎∎∎∎∎∎∎∎∎∎∎∎∎∎∎∎∎∎∎∎∎∎∎∎∎∎

The intent of this application is to determine the failure distribution and to replace components before they enter the wearout phase with its rapidly increasing failure rate pattern.

The first example is the situation where the standard deviation is assumed to be known. In this case the standard deviation will be considered to be 600 hr.

The procedure to calculate the lower limit (tail) of the wearout phase with known standard deviation follows:

1. Determine the reliability required.
2. Determine confidence desired.
3. Obtain the known value for the standard deviation.
4. Determine sample size.
5. Run test and calculate the mean — $\overline{X}$.
6. Calculate the standard error of the mean ($\sigma_{\overline{x}}$), which is $\sigma/\sqrt{n}$
7. Calculate the lower confidence limit for the mean (one-sided limit) as $\overline{X} - Z\,\sigma/\sqrt{n}$. (The value for Z can be found in Table F.)

8. Using the lower confidence limit for the mean, calculate the lower limit for reliability, which is the lower confidence limit for the mean $- Z\sigma$. The values for Z are found in the tables of the normal distribution in Section 23.0.

Example: Determine the time (age) Tw, where a component/system should be replaced to avoid wearout failures at a 99% reliability level with 95% confidence.

1. Reliability required = 0.99 or 99%
2. Confidence level = 0.95 or 95%
3. Standard deviation (σ) = 600
4. Sample size (n) = 16
5. Mean time to wearout $(\hat{M})$ as calculated from test data = 10,000 hr.
6. Standard error of the mean $(\sigma_{\bar{x}})$ = $600/\sqrt{16}$ = 150
7. The lower confidence limit (95%, one tail) for the mean is calculated as $\bar{X} - Z\sigma_{\bar{x}}$. The Z value (see Table F) for one-sided 95% confidence = 1.645. Therefore, $10.000 - 1.645$ (150) = 9753.25 hr, which is the one-sided, lower tail, 95% confidence limit of the mean.
8. Using the value calculated in step 7, calculate the value that 99% (reliability) of the values exceed. The Z value for one tail, lower limit of 0.01 $(1 - .99)$ is 2.326. The .99 reliability point is calculated as:
$9753.25 - (2.326) \times (600) = 9753.25 - 1395.6 = 8357.65$ hr.

The components/systems should be replaced at 8357.65 hr to be 95% confident that 99% of the components/systems will not fail because of wearout causes only.

CASE 2 — STANDARD DEVIATION UNKNOWN ▐▌▐▌▐▌▐▌▐▌▐▌▐▌▐▌▐▌▐▌▐▌▐▌▐▌▐▌▐▌

If the value of the standard deviation is only an estimate, the confidence of this point estimate is dependent upon the sample size, which results in a different approach. The methodology for this case follows:

1. Determine the reliability required.
2. Determine the confidence desired.
3. Determine sample size.
4. Run test and calculate $\bar{X}$ and s.
5. Use the one-sided confidence limit table to determine the 'K' value for required reliability and confidence levels.
6. Calculate the replacement time T_w as $\bar{X} - ks$.

Example: As in the previous example, confidence level = 95% (0.95) and reliability level required = 99% (0.99).
Sample size = 16
Calculated $\bar{X}$ = 10,000 hr
Calculated standard deviation (s) = 600 hr

Using the table of 'K' values for 95% confidence, γ = 0.95 and 99% reliability; sample size = 16 and the 'K' value = 3.463.

The replacement time to prevent wearout failures at 95% confidence and 99% reliability is:

$\overline{X}$ − ks = 10,000 − (3.463) (600)
or 10,000 − (2077.8) = 7922.2 hr

The less that is known about the data (standard deviation unknown), the wider is the prediction interval.

The components/systems should be replaced at 7922.2 hr to be 95% confident that 99% of the components/systems will not fail because of wearout causes only.

Question:

If the MTBF is 60,000 hr, using the data from case 1 (σ known), what is the probability that the system will not fail by either chance or wearout for a use time of 8000 hr?

To calculate the probability of not failing because of either chance cause or wearout, the series system described in Figure 9.1 can be used. The reliability for 8000 hr, $R_{(8000)}$, is calculated for each component of the problem, and the product of these reliabilities is the probability of not failing because of either chance cause or wearout.

From case 1, the lower 95% confidence limit for the mean was found to be 9753.25 hr, and the standard deviation is 600 hr. To determine the probability of surviving 8000 hr without a wearout failure, calculate:

$$Z = \frac{8000 - 9753.25}{600} = -2.922$$

The area under the normal curve above −2.922 is 0.99826. Thus, the probability of surviving up to 8000 hr without a wearout failure using the data from case 1, is 0.99826.

The probability of not failing because of chance cause is given in equation R4 (remember that $\lambda = 1/\Theta$). For this example, the result is:

$$R_{(8000)} \text{ chance cause} = e^{-(8000)\,(0.00001667)} = 0.87517$$

The probability of surviving 8000 hr without either a chance cause failure or a wearout failure is the product of the two calculated reliabilities, which is (0.99826) (0.87517) = 0.873647. It is evident that the probability of failure is increased as an item begins to enter its wearout phase.

15.0 CONDITIONAL PROBABILITY OF FAILURES

In this section the calculation of conditional probabilities will be considered.

Note: Do not use this for exponential calculations during the chance cause failure period.

Sometimes because of scheduling, a system may be required to operate well into its wearout phase (note that chance failures may also occur during this period). For example, if a failure occurs and the impact on the system is not catastrophic, management may want the system to run another 16 hours until a plant shutdown will allow servicing of the system. How can the reliability of the unit (concern here is wearout only) for this time period be calculated? If time of operation to this point is denoted by t_1, the conditional probability can be written as:

$$R_{(t|t>t_1)} = \frac{R(t), \ t>t_1}{R(t_1)}$$

The bearings of an engine have a wearout distribution that is known to be normal. The distribution has a mean wearout time of 2000 hr, and a standard deviation of 25 hr. The time of operation to this point has been 1900 hr. What is the probability that the bearings will survive (wearout failures only) for the next 16 hours?

The conditional probability is written as:

$$R_{(1916 \ hr|t>1900 \ hr)} = \frac{R(1916 \ hr)}{R(1900 \ hr)}$$

The reliability for 1900 hr is calculated as:

$$Z = \left| \frac{1900-2000}{25} \right| = 4 = 0.999968314$$

49

for 1916 hours the result is,

$$Z = \left| \frac{1916-2000}{25} \right| = 3.36 = 0.999610233$$

The probability that the system will operate the next 16 hours without a failure is:

$$\frac{0.999610233}{0.999968314} = 0.9996419$$

or, 99.96% — a reasonable risk to assume.

WEIBULL DISTRIBUTION

One of the most versatile distributions for use in reliability applications is the Weibull distribution. With its many changing shapes the Weibull can be made to fit many distributions. Among these are the Gaussian (normal) and exponential distributions. The calculations for the scale and shape parameters which will be described later are extremely tedious along with being complex. These values of the shape and scale parameters are generally estimated using Weibull graph paper.

In using the Weibull distribution several parameters will be used, which are defined as follows:

β = shape parameter, which determines distribution shape.

η = scale parameter; 63.21% of the values fall below this parameter.

Θ = estimated mean (MTBF estimate in reliability).

$\Gamma(x)$ = gamma function of a variable (x). Values of $\Gamma(x)$ are listed in the gamma function table in Section 23.0, along with the equation for calculating the values of $\Gamma(x)$ for large values of x.

t = noted time of an individual characteristic.

The probability density function for Weibull is:

$$f(t) = \begin{cases} \dfrac{\beta}{\eta} \left(\dfrac{t}{\eta}\right)^{\beta-1} e^{[-(t/\eta)^{\beta}]} & \text{for } t \geq 0 \\ \\ 0 \text{ for } t < 0 \end{cases}$$

and the survival function $P_{(s)}$ is:

$$P_{(s)} = e^{[-(t/\eta)^\beta]}$$

Equation R26: Weibull mean $\mu_w = \eta\Gamma\,(1\,+\,1/\beta)$

Equation R27: Weibull standard deviation $\sigma_w =$

$$\sigma = \eta\sqrt{\Gamma\,(1\,+\,2/\beta)\,-\,\Gamma^2\,(1\,+\,1/\beta)}$$

Example: A unit was tested and the following were the results of the test: $\eta = 20,000$ and $\beta = 2.5$.
Calculate the Weibull mean, standard deviation, and P(s) for 10,000 hr.

Weibull mean estimate $\hat{\mu}_w = 20,000\,\{\Gamma\,(1\,+\,1/2.5)\,\} = 17,746$

Weibull standard deviation estimate $\hat{\sigma}_w =$

$$\hat{\sigma}w = 20,000\,\sqrt{\Gamma\,(1\,+\,2/2.5)\,-\,\Gamma^2\,(1\,+\,1/2.5)} = 7594$$

$$P_{(s)} = {}_e-(10,000/20,000)^{2.5} = 0.838$$

16.1 SHAPE PARAMETER — DISCUSSION ▐▐▐▐▐▐▐▐▐▐▐

The shape parameter (β) is the main influence on distribution shape. When $\Theta = 1$, and the data fit a Weibull distribution with a shape parameter of 3.44, the distribution has the characteristics of the Gaussian distribution. A shape parameter of 1.0 results in an exponential distribution, while $\beta = 2.0$ is a Rayleigh distribution.

16.2 WEIBULL FIT DETERMINATION ▐▐▐▐▐▐▐▐▐▐▐▐▐▐

Weibull graph paper (Figure 16.1) is a means of graphically displaying life tests and failure times. The use of Weibull graph paper gives the means to estimate the shape parameter, scale parameter, and the specified percentage of units surviving or failing at a given time or life.

To plot on Weibull paper, the failure times are placed in ascending order and plotted on the graph paper using a table of median ranks for the appropriate sample size. The best fit line is drawn through the data points, and a parallel line to the best fit line is drawn to determine the shape parameter. The percentage of units expected to survive to a given time is read along the percent axis at the point corresponding with the best fit line. The x axis is the time or cycles to failure.

Example: Twelve items are placed on test with time to failure recorded. The time to failure and median ranks are shown in Table 16.1. Using Weibull graph paper, determine the scale and shape parameters, as well as the time where 40%, 50%, and 80% of units are expected to fail.

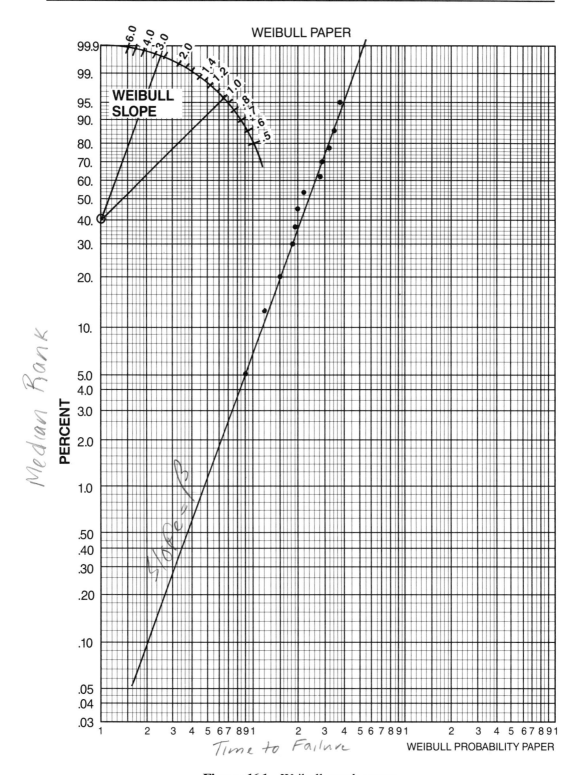

Figure 16.1   Weibull graph paper.

TABLE 16.1

Time to Failure Distribution

Item No.	Time to Failures (hrs) × 100	Median Rank (%)
1	90	5.6
2	116	13.6
3	145	21.7
4	170	29.8
5	185	37.9
6	200	46.0
7	220	54.0
8	265	62.1
9	275	70.2
10	315	78.3
11	335	86.4
12	360	94.4

The graph shows that 40% will fail at about 200 hr, 50% at about 222 hr, and 80% at 310 hr. To determine the value for the shape parameter β, draw a straight line from the center point of the circle (next to the 40 on the left side of the graph) that is parallel to the best fit line drawn through the points on the graph. The point of intersection on the Weibull slope semicircle determines the value for the shape parameter. The scale parameter is about 260 hr, and the shape parameter is about 2.70.

The median rank values are found in the table of median ranks (Table D) in Section 23.0.

To calculate values for median ranks that are not shown in the table, the following formula can be used:

$$MR_{(j)} = \frac{n - j + (0.5)^{1/n}(2j - n - 1)}{n - 1}$$

Where: n = sample size
        j = j_{th} occurrence (failure)

Example: Using the data from this problem, calculate the value of the median rank for the sixth failure in the sample of 12.

$$MR_{(6)} = \frac{12 - 6 + (0.5)^{1/12}[2(6) - 12 - 1]}{11} = 0.4596$$

This value when multiplied by 100 equals 45.96% and has been rounded to 46% in Table 16.1.

17.0 LOG-NORMAL DISTRIBUTION

When working with continuous distributions that show positive skewness, calculations using the Gaussian (normal) distribution prove inadequate. When this situation occurs, and all values are (or transformed to be) > O, taking the natural logs of the values may result in a normal distribution.

For the log-normal distribution:

$$f(x) = \frac{1}{\sigma x \sqrt{2\pi}} \ e^{[-1/2 \ (lnx-\mu/\sigma)^2]} \ , \ x > 0$$

The mean and variance of the log-normal are:

Equation R28: Mean $= e^{[\hat{\mu} + s^2/2]}$

Equation R29: Variance $= [e^{(2\hat{\mu} + s^2)}] \ [e^{s^2} - 1]$

Where $\hat{\mu}$ = mean of the natural logs of individuals.

   s^2 = variance of natural logs of individuals.

Example: Twenty-five measurements are taken of time to failure of a component in hours. The natural logarithms are found to be normally distributed with a mean $\hat{\mu}$ of 3.1 and a variance (s^2) of 1.24 (remember $\hat{\mu}$ and s^2 are for natural log values). Find the untransformed mean and variance in hours.

Mean $= e^{[3.1 + 1.24/2]} = 41.26439$

$$\text{Variance} = [e^{2\,(3.1)\,+\,1.24}]\,[e^{1.24} - 1] =$$
$$[1702.750221]\,[2.4556] \;=\; 4181.2964$$

To calculate tail area probabilities, translated log-normal values are used.

$$Z_{\ln} = \frac{\ln(x) - \hat{\mu}}{s}$$

Where: $\hat{\mu}$ and s are log-normal values.

Example: In the previous example it was found that $\hat{\mu} = 3.1$ and $s = 1.11355$. What percentage will survive 50 hr?

$$Z = \frac{\ln(50) - 3.1}{1.11355} = \frac{3.91202 - 3.1}{1.11355}$$

$Z = 0.7292$. Using the normal Z tables a value of 0.2329 or 23.29% will exceed 50 hr.

18.0 STRESS-STRENGTH INTERFERENCE

Mechanical systems supporting a known or expected stress have usually been designed with a margin of safety. In situations where risk to human life or strategic missions are concerned the risk should be kept low while still maintaining economic justification for the project. One method of calculation used for mechanical designs is stress-strength interference.

Failure will occur when the stress applied exceeds the strength. In Figure 18.1 stress and strength curves do not interfere with each other; the result is no failure.

Figure 18.1   Stress and strength curves that do not interfere with each other result in no failure.

In Figure 18.2 a potential for interference between stress and strength (shaded area) exists. When stress exceeds strength, failure occurs.

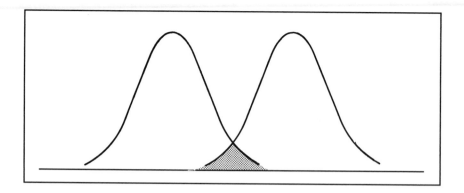

Figure 18.2 When stress exceeds strength (shaded area) failure occurs.

When the stress and strength distributions are independent, the calculations and concepts are straightforward. The following relationship for the curves meeting these restrictions is shown in Figure 18.3. The following equations are used to calculate this relationship:

Equation R30: $\mu_{x\text{-}y} = \mu_x - \mu_y$, which is the mean of the strength-stress distribution.

Equation R31: $\sigma_{x\text{-}y} = \sqrt{\sigma_x^2 + \sigma_y^2}$, which is the standard deviation of the strength-stress distribution.

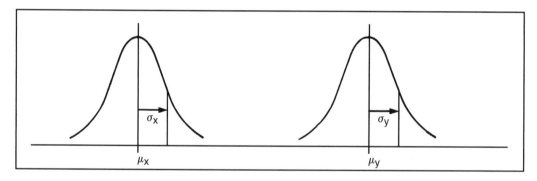

Figure 18.3 Calculations and concepts are straightforward when the stress and strength distributions are independent.

If the x and y distributions are correlated in a manner known to the user with a correlation coefficient, r, the following relationship applies:

Equation R32: $\sigma_{x\text{-}y} = \sqrt{\sigma_x^2 + \sigma_y^2 - 2r\sigma_x\sigma_y}$

If the distributions are log-normal, exponential, gamma, etc., or some combination of these, other equations as found in *Reliability and Engineering Design* by Kapur and Lamberson (1974) will be required. In most cases the relationships given in equations R30 and R31 will be sufficient.

When the stress and strength distributions are normally or near normally distributed for calculating the probability of interference (failure) in Figure 18.2, calculate a Z value and the accompanying area beyond the normal curve Z value from equations R30 and R31 and the following equation results:

Equation R33:
$$Z = \frac{\mu_x - \mu_y}{\sqrt{\sigma_x^2 + \sigma_y^2}}$$

This value is used for the probability value.

Example: Figure 18.4 shows a strength distribution (x) with a mean of 130,000 lbs/sq in and a standard deviation of 11,000 lbs/sq in. The stress distribution (y) has a mean of 100,000 lbs/sq in and a standard deviation of 10,000 lbs/sq in. What is the probability of failure for this configuration?

$$Z = \frac{\mu_x - \mu_y}{\sqrt{\sigma_x^2 + \sigma_y^2}}$$

$$Z = \frac{130,000 - 100,000}{\sqrt{10,000^2 + 11,000^2}} = 2.0180$$

To calculate the probability of failure for Z = 2.0180, determine the area above this Z value using the normal distribution. The area above Z = 0.0218. This means that a probability of approximately 2.18% exists for failure. When the distributions are distinctly non-normal the previous method will not suffice, and other methods as noted earlier will be required.

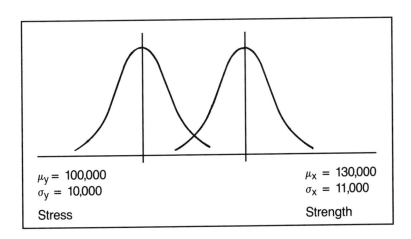

$\mu_y = 100,000$
$\sigma_y = 10,000$

Stress

$\mu_x = 130,000$
$\sigma_x = 11,000$

Strength

Figure 18.4   Strength and stress distributions.

19.0 BINOMIAL CONFIDENCE INTERVALS

For moderate to large sample sizes, the normal distribution can provide an excellent estimate of the confidence limits for the binomial distribution, once a point estimate is made from sample data. While the estimate is accurate, the calculations are somewhat tedious to perform.

The following equations adapted from Burr (1974) can be used with some minor changes in notations for continuity.

The lower limit estimate Φ_L is calculated by:

$$\frac{2r-1+Z^2_{\alpha/2}-Z_{\alpha/2}\sqrt{[(2r-1)(2n-2r+1)/n]+Z^2_{\alpha/2}}}{2(n+Z^2_{\alpha/2})}$$

And the upper limit estimate Φ_U is calculated by:

$$\frac{2r+1+Z^2_{\alpha/2}+Z_{\alpha/2}\sqrt{[(2r+1)(2n-2r-1)/n]+Z^2_{\alpha/2}}}{2(n+Z^2_{\alpha/2})}$$

Where: r   = number of occurrences in the sample
       n   = sample size
       $Z_{\alpha/2}$ = two-sided confidence limit value for the normal distribution

Example: A sample of 75 leptobeam amplifiers found seven to be nonconforming. Calculate the 95% confidence limits for the true fraction nonconforming using these equations.
For this example:
n = 75, r = 7, $Z_{\alpha/2}$ = 1.96.

$\Phi_L =$

$$\frac{(2\times7) - 1 + 1.96^2 - 1.96 \sqrt{[\,(\,(2)\,(7) - 1\,)\,)\,(\,(2)\,(75) - (2)\,(7) + 1)\,/75] + 1.96^2}}{2\,(75 + 1.96^2)}$$

$= 0.041519$

$\Phi_U =$

$$\frac{(2\times7) + 1 + 1.96^2 + 1.96 \sqrt{[\,(\,(2)\,(7) + 1\,)\,)\,(\,(2)\,(75) - (2)\,(7) + 1)\,/75] + 1.96^2}}{2\,(75 + 1.96^2)}$$

$= 0.18852$

The 95% confidence interval for the fraction nonconforming is 0.0415 to 0.1885. This is compared to the simple point estimate of $7/75 = 0.09333$.

20.0 CHI-SQUARE APPROXIMATION FOR POISSON CONFIDENCE INTERVALS

The relationship (Nelson, 1989) between the chi-square distribution and the Poisson distribution allows for simple calculations of Poisson confidence intervals. To calculate the upper confidence limit for number of occurrences, calculate the appropriate degrees of freedom (df) for the chi-square table as $\nu = 2 (r + 1)$. To calculate the lower confidence limit for number of occurrences calculate the df as 2r.

When calculating 90% two-sided confidence intervals, use the columns labelled 0.05 and 0.95, as well as the appropriate df for upper and lower confidence limits. The value obtained from the chi-square table (Table B) is divided by 2 for the required estimate.

Example: An examination of a Poisson distribution noted 13 occurrences. Find the 90% confidence interval for the number of occurrences.

Upper confidence limit df $= 2 (13 + 1) = 28$. The chi-square table value for 28 df and $\alpha = 0.05$ is 41.337. The upper confidence limit $= 41.337/2 = 20.67$.

Lower confidence limit df $= 2 (13) = 26$. The chi-square table value for 26 df and $1 - \alpha = 0.95$ is 15.379. The lower confidence limit $= 15.379/2 = 7.690$.

Thus, the 90% confidence interval for number of occurrences is 7.66 to 20.67.

ARRHENIUS MODEL

Implicit in the increasing failure rates for increased temperatures is an effect referred to as the Arrhenius model. The Arrhenius equation as given by Shooman (1968) is:

Equation R34: $Q^*(x) = \dfrac{dQ(x)}{dt} = e^{A-B/x} = e^A e^{-B/x}$

Where: The quantity changing is Q and its time derivative is Q*.
x is a stress parameter fixing Q.
A and B are constants.

O'Conner (1981) provides a different equation to describe the change in the process rate, which drives the failure rate, provided by the Arrhenius model. The equation provided by O'Conner is:

Equation R35: $\lambda_b = K \exp(-E/kt)$

Where: λ_b is the base failure rate of the item
E is the activation energy (eV) for the process
k is Boltzmann's constant, 8.63×10^{-4} eV K^{-1}
T is the absolute temperature (K)
K is a constant

The value of K (the constant) depends upon a variety of factors and will not be fully developed here. Instead, examples from MIL-HDBK-217 will be used to illustrate the change in failure rate when the temperature is increased.

Example 1: A MIL-S-19500 diode, group IV, germanium, has a failure rate at 70% stress level of 0.0077 per 10^6 hr at 30°C. At 40°C the failure rate increases to 0.013 for an increase of 69%. The 10°C increase in temperature resulted in a failure rate 1.69 times the value at 30°C. At the 80% stress level, the failure rate at 30°C is 0.011 per 10^6 hr. At 40°C, the failure rate is 0.024 per 10^6 hr, for an increase of 118%. The failure rate was slightly more than doubled resulting from the change in temperature of 10°C.

Example 2: Capacitors, vacuum or gas, fixed or variable, T $=$ 125°C max. rated. At 50% stress level, the failure rate at 100°C is 0.68 per 10^6 hr, while at 110°C, the failure rate is 0.87 failures per 10^6 hr. The 110°C failure rate is 1.28 times the 100° failure rate. At 120°C, the failure rate is 1.2 failures per 10^6 hr, for an increase of 40% over the 110°C failure rate.

GENERAL RULE ▌▌▌

The casual rule of thumb for the Arrhenius effect states that for every 10°C increase in temperature, the chemical reactions for electronic and electrical components double, along with their respective failure rates. The examples cited here show that this is only a general rule which should be tempered with experience. It is obvious by this model that even small increases in temperature have dramatic increases in failure rates.

22.0 SEQUENTIAL TESTING

22.1 INTRODUCTION

Sequential testing is not a method for estimating MTBF values; rather, sequential testing is a situation wherein the results are continually reassessed for making a decision with the minimum amount of testing. The hypothesis and decision points as well as the actions taken for these points are:

Null hypothesis - H_O: $\Theta = \Theta_0$
Alternative hypothesis - H_A: $\Theta \leq \Theta_1$

Decisions made based on the results of the test include:

A. Accept the null hypothesis that the actual MTBF (Θ) meets or exceeds the acceptable MTBF and accept the lot.

B. Reject the null hypothesis that the actual MTBF (Θ) meets or exceeds the acceptable MTBF in favor of the alternative hypothesis that the actual MTBF is equal to or less than the unacceptable MTBF and reject the lot.

C. Continue testing, because enough information is not available to either accept the null hypothesis or reject the null hypothesis in favor of the alternative hypothesis.

The operating curve (OC curve) for sequential testing is determined before testing by specifying four values. These values are shown with the OC curve in Figure 22.1. The values of Θ_0, Θ_1, α, β, are specified when designing the sequential test procedure.

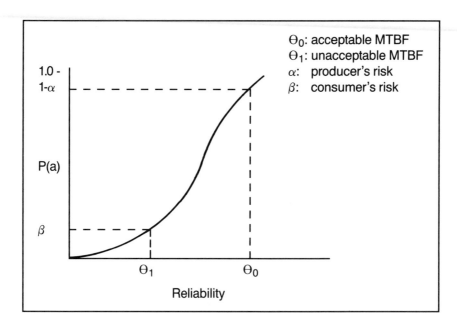

Figure 22.1 Occurrence (OC) curve showing the four values of Θ_0, Θ_1, α, and β.

Θ_0: The acceptable reliability
α: Level of significance (producers risk of rejecting when Θ_0 is true)
Θ_1: The unacceptable reliability
β: Consumers risk (probability of acceptance when Θ_1 is true)

Once the test is designed and the pertinent values are calculated, a graph of the sequential test is constructed that has the three areas as shown in Figure 22.2.

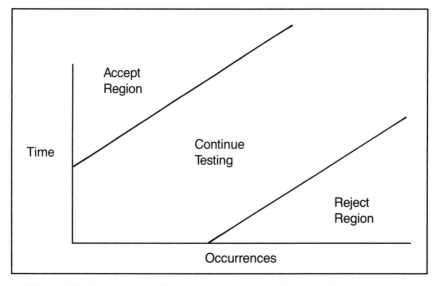

Figure 22.2 A graph of the sequential test showing the three areas.

22.2 SEQUENTIAL TESTING WHEN THE EXPONENTIAL DISTRIBUTION IS APPROPRIATE ▮▮▮▮▮▮▮▮▮▮▮▮▮▮

The underlying distribution for time-to-failure can be assumed to be exponential.

22.2.1 ACCUMULATING TOTAL TEST TIME ▮▮▮▮▮▮▮▮▮▮▮▮▮▮▮▮▮

Items may be tested individually in a sequential fashion or (n) items can be tested simultaneously.

T = Total unit test time
r = Number of failures
t_i = Time to failure for ith unit
Θ = the MTBF reliability goal

The values of Θ_0, Θ_1, α, and β, must be specified, and $\Theta_1 < \Theta_0$. The relationship of these values is shown on the graph in Figure 22.3.

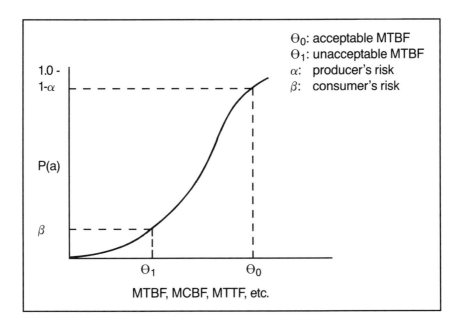

Figure 22.3 Operating characteristic curve for sequential sampling plan.

SEQUENTIAL EQUATION ▮▮

Calculate the following:

$D = (1/\Theta_1 - 1/\Theta_0), \Theta_1 < \Theta_0$
$s = 1/D \ln (\Theta_0/\Theta_1)$
$h_1 = 1/D \ln \{(1-\beta)/\alpha\}$
$h_0 = 1/D \ln \{ (1-\alpha)/\beta\}$

Then the sequential formula is:

$$rs - h_1 \leq T \leq rs + h_0$$

Example: Items are to be placed on test. The following requirements apply:

$$\Theta_0 = 12{,}000$$
$$\Theta_1 = 4000$$
$$\alpha = 0.05$$
$$\beta = 0.10$$

Calculate the test parameters and draw the test graph using the following equations:

Equation R36: $D = (1/\Theta_1 - 1/\Theta_0)$, $\Theta_1 < \Theta_0$

Equation R37: $s = slope = 1/D \ln (\Theta_0/\Theta_1)$

Equation R38: h_1 = Y intercept for reject line
$$= 1/D \ln \{ (1-\beta)/\alpha \}$$

Equation R39: h_0 = Y intercept for accept line
$$= 1/D \ln \{ (1-\alpha)/\beta \}$$

The formulae for the decision lines are:

Equation R40: Reject line $= rs - h_1 \leq T$

Equation R41: Accept line $= rs + h_0 \geq T$
Where r is the number of failures.

Using R36 through R41 the following is derived:

$$D = [1/4000 - 1/12000] = 0.000166667$$

$$s = [1/0.000167 \ln (12000/4000)] = 6591.6737$$

$$h_1 = [1/0.000167 \ln (0.90/0.05)] = (17342.1959)\,(-1) = -17342.1959$$

$$h_0 = [1/0.000167 \ln (0.95/0.10)] = 13{,}507.7481$$

Note: The value of h_1 was multiplied by the value of -1, as the Y intercept for the reject line must fall below the Y intercept of the accept line. The value of h_1 remains unchanged for all other calculations. The graph is shown in Figure 22.4. Figure 22.4 is drawn from the calculated points shown in Table 22.1 calculated for this example.

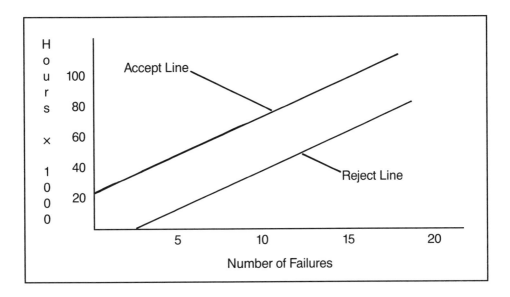

Figure 22.4 The Y intercept for the reject line must fall below the Y intercept of the accept line.

TABLE 22.1

Values for Plotting Points for Accept and Reject Lines Drawn in Figure 22.4

Number of Failures	Points for Accept Line	Points for Reject Line
4	39,874.44	9,024.50
6	53,057.79	22,207.88
8	66,241.14	35,391.19

22.3 ACCUMULATING FAILURES ▮▮▮▮▮▮▮▮▮▮▮▮▮▮▮▮▮▮▮▮▮▮▮▮

In this situation the underlying time to failure distribution is assumed to be exponential. Test time and failures are being accumulated on several units. The number of units can be varied on test at will.

The test goal is stated as a failure rate λ, or, MTBF. The values of λ_0, λ_1, α, and β must be specified to run the test. The relationship between these quantities is shown in Figure 22.5, and the accept/reject graph is shown in Figure 22.6.

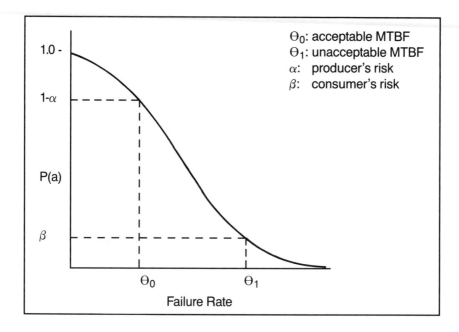

Figure 22.5 Relationship between quantities for total accumulated test time and number of failures.

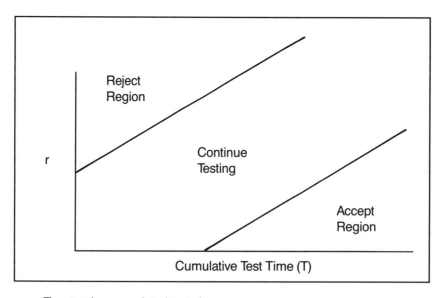

T = total accumulated test time
r = total accumulated number of failures

Figure 22.6 Accept/reject graph for Figure 22.5.

SEQUENTIAL VALUES ||||||||||||||||||||||||||||||||||||||||||||||||||||||

Before performing the test, calculate:

$D = \ln(\lambda_1/\lambda_0), \quad \lambda_0 < \lambda_1$

$s = 1/D\,(\lambda_1 - \lambda_0)$

$h_0 = 1/D\,\ln\{(1-\alpha)/\beta\}$

$h_1 = 1/D\,\ln\{(1-\beta)/\alpha\}$

Thus, the sequential equation is:

$sT - h_0 \leq r \leq sT + h_1$

22.4 USE OF THE WEIBULL DISTRIBUTION FOR SEQUENTIAL TESTING ||||||||||||||||||||||||||||||||

When using the Weibull distribution in sequential testing the Weibull shape parameter (β) is assumed to be known. The reliability goal is expressed in terms of the characteristic life or Θ.

The values α, Θ_0, δ, and Θ_1 must be specified to run the test. The reason for using σ as the symbol for consumer's risk rather than β, is that the symbol β is used in the equations and stands for shape parameter. The symbol is different, but the meaning as consumer's risk is the same. These values are related as shown in Figure 22.7. Note that $\Theta_1 < \Theta_0$.

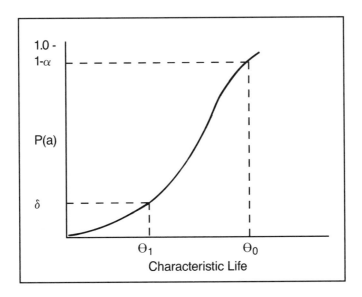

Figure 22.7 Values as used in the Weibull distribution for sequential testing.

SEQUENTIAL FORMULAE IIIIIIIIIIIIIIIIIIIIIIIIIIIIIIIIIIIIIIIIIIIIIIIIIIIIIIIIIIIIIII

The following values must be calculated:

$$D = 1/\Theta_1^\beta - 1/\Theta_0^\beta, \ \Theta_1 < \Theta_0$$

$$b = \frac{1}{D} \ \beta \ln (\Theta_0/\Theta_1)$$

$$h_0 = \frac{1}{D} \ \ln \left(\frac{1-\delta}{\alpha}\right)$$

$$h_1 = \frac{1}{D} \ \ln \left(\frac{1-\alpha}{\delta}\right)$$

Thus the sequential equation is:

$$nb - h_0 \leq \sum_{i=1}^{n} t_i^\beta \leq nb + h_1$$

Example: For a given application, it is reasonable to assume a Weibull distribution with β = 2.0. The test parameters are: $\Theta_0 = 1000$ hr, $\Theta_1 = 600$ hr, $\delta = 0.25$, $\alpha = 0.10$. Develop the equation for the sequential sampling plan.

$$D = \frac{1}{600^2} - \frac{1}{1000^2} = 0.00000178$$

$$b = \frac{1}{0.00000178} \times \ln \left(\frac{1000}{600}\right) = 287,339.4$$

$$h_0 = \frac{1}{0.00000178} \times \ln \left(\frac{0.75}{0.10}\right) = 1,133,382.95$$

$$h_1 = \frac{1}{0.00000178} \times \ln \left(\frac{0.90}{0.25}\right) = 720,525.29$$

The sequential equation for this example is:

$$n \ (287,339.4) - 1,133,382.95 \leq \sum_{i=1}^{n} t_i^2 \leq n \ (287,339.4) + 720,525.29$$

23.0 TABLES

TABLE A

Beta Table*

Fixed Sample Size (n) and Confidence Level (γ): Reliability (p) Assessed as a Function of Number of Successes (s) or the Number of Failures (r)

n	s	r	.5	.75	.90	.95	.99	.995
1	0	1	.293	.134	.051	.025	.005	.002
	1	0	.707	.500	.316	.224	.100	.071
2	0	2	.206	.092	.034	.017	.003	.002
	1	1	.500	.326	.196	.135	.059	.041
	2	0	.794	.630	.464	.368	.216	.171
3	1	2	.386	.243	.142	.098	.042	.029
	2	1	.614	.456	.320	.249	.141	.111
	3	0	.841	.707	.562	.473	.316	.266
4	2	2	.500	.359	.247	.189	.106	.083
	3	1	.686	.546	.416	.343	.222	.185
	4	0	.871	.758	.631	.549	.398	.346
5	3	2	.579	.447	.794	.271	.173	.144
	4	1	.736	.610	.333	.418	.294	.254
	5	0	.891	.794	.681	.607	.464	.414
6	4	2	.636	.514	.404	.341	.236	.203
	5	1	.772	.659	.547	.479	.357	.315
	6	0	.906	.820	.720	.652	.518	.469
7	5	2	.679	.567	.462	.400	.293	.258
	6	1	.799	.697	.594	.529	.410	.368
	7	0	.917	.841	.750	.688	.562	.516
8	6	2	.714	.609	.510	.450	.344	.307
	7	1	.820	.728	.632	.571	.456	.415
	8	0	.926	.857	.774	.717	.600	.555

* Reproduced by permission of M.O. Locks, *Reliability, Maintainability, and Availability Assessment,* Rochell Park, NJ: Spartan Books, 1973.

TABLE A (cont.)

Beta Table*

Fixed Sample Size (n) and Confidence Level (γ): Reliability (p) Assessed as a Function of Number of Successes (s) or the Number of Failures (r)

n	s	r	.5	.75	.90	.95	.99	.995
9	7	2	.742	.645	.550	.493	.388	.352
	8	1	.838	.753	.663	.606	.496	.456
	9	0	.933	.871	.794	.741	.631	.589
10	7	3	.676	.580	.489	.436	.340	.307
	8	2	.764	.674	.585	.530	.428	.392
	9	1	.852	.773	.690	.636	.530	.492
	10	0	.939	.882	.811	.762	.658	.618
12	9	3	.725	.638	.556	.505	.412	.379
	10	2	.800	.720	.640	.590	.494	.459
	11	1	.874	.806	.732	.684	.587	.551
	12	0	.948	.899	.838	.794	.702	.665
15	12	3	.775	.702	.629	.583	.497	.466
	13	2	.836	.769	.700	.656	.570	.537
	14	1	.897	.840	.778	.736	.651	.619
	15	0	.958	.917	.866	.829	.750	.718
20	17	3	.828	.769	.709	.671	.596	.568
	18	2	.875	.822	.766	.729	.656	.628
	19	1	.921	.877	.827	.793	.723	.696
	20	0	.968	.936	.896	.867	.803	.777
25	22	3	.861	.811	.761	.728	.663	.638
	23	2	.898	.855	.808	.777	.714	.690
	24	1	.936	.900	.858	.830	.771	.747
	25	0	.974	.948	.915	.891	.838	.816
30	27	3	.883	.841	.797	.768	.711	.689
	28	2	.915	.877	.837	.810	.755	.734
	29	1	.946	.916	.880	.856	.804	.784
	30	0	.978	.956	.928	.908	.862	.843

*Reproduced by permission of M.O. Locks, *Reliability, Maintainability, and Availability Assessment,* Rochell Park, NJ: Spartan Books, 1973.

TABLE A (cont.)

Beta Table*

Fixed Sample Size (n) and Confidence Level (γ): Reliability (p) Assessed as a Function of Number of Successes (s) or the Number of Failures (r)

n	s	r	.5	.75	.90	.95	.99	.995
35	31	4	.871	.831	.791	.764	.710	.690
	32	3	.899	.862	.824	.798	.747	.727
	33	2	.926	.894	.859	.835	.786	.767
	34	1	.954	.927	.896	.875	.829	.811
	35	0	.981	.962	.938	.920	.880	.863
40	36	4	.887	.851	.814	.790	.742	.724
	37	3	.911	.879	.844	.822	.775	.757
	38	2	.935	.907	.875	.854	.810	.793
	39	1	.959	.936	.908	.889	.849	.832
	40	0	.983	.967	.945	.930	.894	.879
45	41	4	.899	.867	.834	.812	.768	.751
	42	3	.921	.892	.860	.840	.798	.781
	43	2	.942	.917	.888	.869	.830	.814
	44	1	.964	.942	.918	.901	.864	.849
	45	0	.985	.970	.951	.937	.905	.891
50	46	4	.909	.880	.849	.829	.789	.773
	47	3	.928	.902	.874	.855	.816	.801
	48	2	.948	.925	.899	.882	.845	.831
	49	1	.967	.948	.926	.910	.877	.863
	50	0	.985	.973	.956	.943	.914	.901
60	56	4	.924	.899	.873	.856	.821	.808
	57	3	.940	.918	.894	.878	.845	.831
	58	2	.956	.937	.915	.900	.869	.857

*Reproduced by permission of M.O. Locks, *Reliability, Maintainability, and Availability Assessment,* Rochell Park, NJ: Spartan Books, 1973.

TABLE A (cont.)

Beta Table*

Fixed Sample Size (n) and Confidence Level (γ): Reliability (p) Assessed as a Function of Number of Successes (s) or the Number of Failures (r)

n	s	r	.5	.75	.90	.95	.99	.995
	59	1	.973	.956	.938	.925	.896	.884
	60	0	.989	.978	.963	.952	.927	.917
75	71	4	.939	.919	.898	.884	.855	.843
	72	3	.952	.934	.914	.901	.874	.863
	73	2	.965	.949	.932	.920	.894	.884
	74	1	.978	.965	.950	.939	.916	.906
	75	0	.991	.982	.970	.961	.941	.933
100	95	5	.944	.928	.910	.899	.875	.866
	96	4	.954	.939	.922	.912	.889	.880
	97	3	.964	.950	.935	.925	.904	.896
	98	2	.974	.962	.948	.939	.919	.911
	99	1	.983	.974	.962	.954	.936	.929
	100	0	.993	.986	.978	.971	.955	.949
150	145	5	.962	.951	.939	.932	.916	.909
	146	4	.969	.959	.948	.940	.925	.919
	147	3	.976	.966	.956	.950	.935	.929
	148	2	.982	.974	.965	.959	.946	.940
	149	1	.989	.982	.974	.969	.957	.952
	150	0	.996	.991	.985	.980	.970	.966
200	195	5	.972	.963	.954	.948	.963	.931
	196	4	.977	.969	.961	.955	.943	.939
	197	3	.982	.975	.967	.962	.951	.946
	198	2	.987	.981	.974	.969	.959	.955
	199	1	.992	.987	.981	.977	.967	.964
	200	0	.996	.993	.989	.985	.977	.974

*Reproduced by permission of M.O. Locks, *Reliability, Maintainability, and Availability Assessment,* Rochell Park, NJ: Spartan Books, 1973.

TABLE B
Distribution of Chi-Square

df	0.99	0.98	0.95	0.90	0.80	0.70	0.50	0.30	0.20	0.10	0.05	0.02	0.01	0.001
1	0.0157	0.0628	0.00393	0.0158	0.0642	0.148	0.455	1.074	1.642	2.706	3.841	5.412	6.635	10.827
2	0.0201	0.0404	0.103	0.211	0.446	0.713	1.386	2.408	3.219	4.605	5.991	7.824	9.210	13.815
3	0.115	0.185	0.352	0.584	1.005	1.424	2.366	3.665	4.642	6.251	7.815	9.837	11.341	16.268
4	0.297	0.429	0.711	1.064	1.649	2.195	3.357	4.878	5.989	7.779	9.488	11.668	13.277	18.465
5	0.554	0.752	1.145	1.610	2.343	3.000	4.351	6.064	7.289	9.236	11.070	13.388	15.086	20.517
6	0.872	1.134	1.635	2.204	3.070	3.828	5.348	7.231	8.558	10.645	12.592	15.033	16.812	22.457
7	1.239	1.564	2.167	2.833	3.822	4.671	6.346	8.383	9.803	12.017	14.067	16.622	18.475	24.322
8	1.646	2.032	2.733	3.490	4.594	5.527	7.344	9.524	11.030	13.362	15.507	18.168	20.090	26.125
9	2.088	2.532	3.325	4.168	5.380	6.393	8.343	10.656	12.242	14.684	16.919	19.679	21.666	27.877
10	2.558	3.059	3.940	4.865	6.179	7.267	9.342	11.781	13.442	15.987	18.307	21.161	23.209	29.588
11	3.053	3.609	4.575	5.578	6.989	8.148	10.341	12.899	14.631	17.275	19.675	22.618	24.725	31.264
12	3.571	4.178	5.226	6.304	7.807	9.034	11.340	14.011	15.812	18.549	21.026	24.054	26.217	32.909
13	4.107	4.765	5.892	7.042	8.634	9.926	12.340	15.119	16.985	19.812	22.362	25.472	27.688	34.528
14	4.660	5.368	6.571	7.790	9.467	10.821	13.339	16.222	18.151	21.064	23.685	26.873	29.141	36.123
15	5.229	5.985	7.261	8.547	10.307	11.721	14.339	17.322	19.311	22.307	24.996	28.259	30.578	37.697
16	5.812	6.614	7.962	9.312	11.152	12.624	15.338	18.418	20.465	23.542	26.296	29.663	32.000	39.252
17	6.408	7.255	8.762	10.085	12.002	13.531	16.338	19.511	21.615	24.769	27.587	30.995	33.409	40.790
18	7.015	7.906	9.390	10.865	12.857	14.440	17.338	20.601	22.760	25.989	28.869	32.346	34.805	42.312
19	7.633	8.567	10.117	11.651	13.716	15.352	18.338	21.689	23.900	27.204	30.144	33.687	36.191	43.820
20	8.260	9.237	10.851	12.443	14.578	16.266	19.337	22.775	25.038	28.412	31.410	35.020	37.566	45.315
21	8.897	9.915	11.591	13.240	15.445	17.182	20.337	23.858	26.171	29.615	32.671	36.343	38.932	46.797
22	9.542	10.600	12.338	14.041	16.314	18.101	21.337	24.939	27.301	30.813	33.924	37.659	40.289	48.268
23	10.196	11.293	13.091	14.848	17.187	19.021	22.337	26.018	28.429	32.007	35.172	38.968	41.638	49.728
24	10.856	11.992	13.848	15.659	18.062	19.943	23.337	27.096	29.553	33.196	36.415	40.270	42.980	51.179
25	11.524	12.697	14.611	16.473	18.940	20.867	24.337	28.172	30.675	34.382	37.652	41.566	44.314	52.620
26	12.198	13.409	15.379	17.292	19.820	21.792	25.336	29.246	31.795	35.563	38.885	42.856	45.642	54.052
27	12.879	14.125	16.151	18.114	20.703	22.719	26.336	30.319	32.912	36.741	40.113	44.140	46.963	55.476
28	13.565	14.847	16.928	18.939	21.588	23.647	27.336	31.391	34.027	37.916	41.337	45.419	48.278	56.893
29	14.256	15.574	17.708	19.768	22.475	24.577	28.336	32.461	35.139	39.087	42.557	46.693	49.588	58.302
30	14.953	16.306	18.493	20.599	23.364	25.508	29.336	33.530	36.250	40.256	43.773	47.962	50.892	59.703

TABLE C

Gamma Function of Γ (x)

x	Γ(x)	x	Γ(x)
1.00	1.000000	1.26	0.904397
1.01	.994326	1.27	.902503
1.02	.988844	1.28	.900718
1.03	.983550	1.29	.899042
1.04	.978438	1.30	.897471
1.05	.973504	1.31	.896004
1.06	.968744	1.32	.894640
1.07	.964152	1.33	.893378
1.08	.959725	1.34	.892216
1.09	.955459	1.35	.891151
1.10	.951351	1.36	.890185
1.11	.947396	1.37	.889314
1.12	.943590	1.38	.888537
1.13	.939931	1.39	.887854
1.14	.936416	1.40	.887264
1.15	.933041	1.41	.886756
1.16	.929803	1.42	.886356
1.17	.926700	1.43	.886036
1.18	.923728	1.44	.885805
1.19	.920885	1.45	.885661
1.20	.918169	1.46	.885604
1.21	.915576	1.47	.885633
1.22	.913106	1.48	.885747
1.23	.910755	1.49	.885945
1.24	.908521	1.50	.886227
1.25	.906402	1.51	.886592

TABLE C (cont.)

x	$\Gamma(x)$	x	$\Gamma(x)$
1.52	.887037	1.78	.926227
1.53	.887568	1.79	.928767
1.54	.888178	1.80	.931384
1.55	.888868	1.81	.934076
1.56	.889639	1.82	.936845
1.57	.890490	1.83	.939690
1.58	.891420	1.84	.942612
1.59	.892428	1.85	.945611
1.60	.893515	1.86	.948687
1.61	.894681	1.87	.951840
1.62	.895924	1.88	.955071
1.63	.897244	1.89	.958379
1.64	.898642	1.90	.961766
1.65	.900117	1.91	.965231
1.66	.901668	1.92	.968774
1.67	.903296	1.93	.972397
1.68	.905001	1.94	.976099
1.69	.906782	1.95	.979881
1.70	.908639	1.96	.983743
1.71	.910572	1.97	.987685
1.72	.912581	1.98	.991708
1.73	.914665	1.99	.995813
1.74	.916826	2.00	1.000000
1.75	.919063		
1.76	.921375		
1.77	.923763		

For larger values of $\Gamma(x)$, $\Gamma(x+1) = x\Gamma(x)$.
EX: $\Gamma(2.3) = 1.3\,(.897471) = 1.166712$

TABLE D

Median Rank Values

SAMPLE SIZE

RANK ORDER	1	2	3	4	5	6	7	8	9	10
1	50.0	29.3	20.6	15.9	12.9	10.9	9.4	8.3	7.4	6.7
2		70.7	50.0	38.6	31.4	26.4	22.8	20.1	18.0	16.2
3			79.4	61.4	50.0	42.1	36.4	32.1	28.6	25.9
4				84.1	68.6	57.9	50.0	44.0	39.3	35.5
5					87.1	73.6	63.6	56.0	50.0	45.2
6						89.1	77.2	67.9	60.7	54.8
7							90.6	79.9	71.4	64.5
8								91.7	82.0	74.1
9									92.6	83.8
10										93.3

SAMPLE SIZE

RANK ORDER	11	12	13	14	15	16	17	18	19	20
1	6.1	5.6	5.2	4.8	4.5	4.2	4.0	3.8	3.6	3.4
2	14.8	13.6	12.6	11.7	10.9	10.3	9.7	9.2	8.7	8.3
3	23.6	21.7	20.0	18.6	17.4	16.4	15.4	14.6	13.8	13.1
4	32.4	29.8	27.5	25.6	23.9	22.5	21.2	20.0	19.0	18.1
5	41.2	37.9	35.0	32.6	30.5	28.6	26.9	25.5	24.2	23.0
6	50.0	46.0	42.5	39.5	37.0	34.7	32.7	30.9	29.3	27.9
7	58.8	54.0	50.0	46.5	43.5	40.8	38.5	36.4	34.5	32.8
8	67.6	62.1	57.5	53.5	50.0	46.9	44.2	41.8	39.7	37.7
9	76.4	70.2	65.0	60.5	56.5	53.1	50.0	47.3	44.8	42.6
10	85.2	78.3	72.5	67.4	63.0	59.2	55.8	52.7	50.0	47.5
11	93.9	86.4	80.0	74.4	69.5	65.3	61.5	58.2	55.2	52.5
12		94.4	87.4	81.4	76.1	71.4	67.3	63.6	60.3	57.4
13			94.8	88.3	82.6	77.5	73.1	69.1	65.5	62.3
14				95.2	89.1	83.6	78.8	74.5	70.7	67.2
15					95.5	89.7	84.6	80.0	75.8	72.1
16						95.8	90.3	85.4	81.0	77.0
17							96.0	90.8	86.2	81.9
18								96.2	91.3	86.9
19									96.4	91.7
20										96.6

TABLE D (cont.)

SAMPLE SIZE

RANK ORDER	21	22	23	24	25	26	27	28	29	30
1	3.2	3.1	3.0	2.8	2.7	2.6	2.5	2.4	2.4	2.3
2	7.9	7.5	7.2	6.9	6.6	6.4	6.1	5.9	5.7	5.5
3	12.5	12.0	11.5	11.0	10.6	10.2	9.8	9.4	9.1	8.8
4	17.2	16.4	15.7	15.1	14.5	13.9	13.4	13.0	12.5	12.1
5	21.9	20.9	20.0	19.2	18.4	17.7	17.1	16.5	15.9	15.4
6	26.6	25.4	24.3	23.3	22.4	21.5	20.7	20.0	19.3	18.7
7	31.3	29.9	28.6	27.4	26.3	25.3	24.4	23.5	22.7	22.0
8	35.9	34.3	32.9	31.5	30.3	29.1	28.1	27.1	26.1	25.3
9	40.6	38.8	37.1	35.6	34.2	32.9	31.7	30.6	29.6	28.6
10	45.3	43.3	41.4	39.7	38.2	36.7	35.4	34.1	33.0	31.9
11	50.0	47.8	45.7	43.8	42.1	40.5	39.0	37.7	36.4	35.2
12	54.7	52.2	50.0	47.9	46.1	44.3	42.7	41.2	39.8	38.5
13	59.4	56.7	54.3	52.1	50.0	48.1	46.3	44.7	43.2	41.8
14	64.1	61.2	58.6	56.2	53.9	51.9	50.0	48.2	46.6	45.1
15	68.7	65.7	62.9	60.3	57.9	55.7	53.7	51.8	50.0	48.4
16	73.4	70.1	67.1	64.4	61.8	59.5	57.3	55.3	53.4	51.6
17	78.1	74.6	71.4	68.5	65.8	63.3	61.0	58.8	56.8	54.9
18	82.8	79.1	75.7	72.6	69.7	67.1	64.6	62.4	60.2	58.2
19	87.5	83.6	80.0	76.7	73.7	70.9	68.3	65.9	63.6	61.5
20	92.1	88.0	84.3	80.8	77.6	74.7	71.9	69.4	67.0	64.9
21	96.8	92.5	88.5	84.9	81.6	78.5	75.6	72.9	70.4	68.1
22		96.9	92.8	89.0	85.5	82.3	79.3	76.5	73.9	71.4
23			97.0	93.1	89.4	86.1	82.9	80.0	77.3	74.7
24				97.2	93.4	89.8	86.6	83.5	80.7	78.0
25					97.3	93.6	90.2	87.0	84.1	81.3
26						97.4	93.9	90.6	87.5	84.6
27							97.5	94.1	90.9	87.9
28								97.6	94.3	91.2
29									97.6	94.5
30										97.9

TABLE E

Normal Distribution

AREA BELOW Z

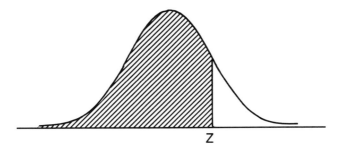

Z

Z	.00	.01	.02	.03	.04	.05	.06	.07	.08	.09
0.0	.5000	.5040	.5080	.5120	.5160	.5199	.5239	.5279	.5319	.5359
.1	.5398	.5438	.5478	.5517	.5557	.5596	.5636	.5674	.5714	.5753
.2	.5793	.5832	.5871	.5910	.5948	.5987	.6026	.6064	.6103	.6141
.3	.6179	.6217	.6255	.6293	.6331	.6368	.6406	.6443	.6480	.6517
.4	.6554	.6519	.6628	.6664	.6700	.6736	.6772	.6808	.6844	.6879
.5	.6915	.6950	.6985	.7019	.7054	.7088	.7123	.7157	.7190	.7224
.6	.7257	.7291	.7324	.7357	.7389	.7422	.7454	.7486	.7517	.7549
.7	.7580	.7611	.7642	.7673	.7704	.7734	.7764	.7794	.7823	.7852
.8	.7881	.7910	.7939	.7967	.7995	.8023	.8051	.8078	.8106	.8133
.9	.8159	.8186	.8212	.8238	.8264	.8289	.8315	.8340	.8365	.8389
1.0	.8413	.8438	.8461	.8485	.8508	.8531	.8554	.8577	.8599	.8621
1.1	.8643	.8665	.8686	.8708	.8729	.8749	.8770	.8790	.8810	.8830
1.2	.8849	.8869	.8888	.8907	.8925	.8944	.8962	.8980	.8997	.9015
1.3	.9032	.9049	.9066	.9082	.9099	.9115	.9131	.9147	.9162	.9177
1.4	.9192	.9207	.9222	.9236	.9251	.9265	.9279	.9292	.9306	.9319
1.5	.9332	.9345	.9357	.9370	.9382	.9394	.9406	.9418	.9429	.9441
1.6	.9452	.9463	.9474	.9484	.9495	.9505	.9515	.9525	.9535	.9545
1.7	.9554	.9564	.9573	.9582	.9591	.9599	.9608	.9616	.9625	.9633
1.8	.9641	.9649	.9656	.9664	.9671	.9678	.9686	.9693	.9699	.9706
1.9	.9713	.9719	.9726	.9732	.9738	.9744	.9750	.9756	.9761	.9767
2.0	.9772	.9778	.9783	.9788	.9793	.9798	.9803	.9808	.9812	.9817
2.1	.9821	.9826	.9830	.9834	.9838	.9842	.9846	.9850	.9954	.9857
2.2	.9861	.9864	.9868	.9871	.9875	.9878	.9881	.9884	.9887	.9890
2.3	.9893	.9896	.9898	.9901	.9904	.9906	.9909	.9911	.9913	.9916
2.4	.9918	.9920	.9922	.9925	.9927	.9929	.9931	.9932	.9934	.9936
2.5	.9938	.9940	.9941	.9943	.9945	.9946	.9948	.9949	.9951	.9952
2.6	.9953	.9955	.9956	.9957	.9959	.9960	.9961	.9962	.9963	.9964
2.7	.9965	.9966	.9967	.9968	.9969	.9970	.9971	.9972	.9973	.9974
2.8	.9974	.9975	.9976	.9977	.9977	.9978	.9979	.9979	.9980	.9981
2.9	.9981	.9982	.9982	.9983	.9984	.9984	.9985	.9985	.9986	.9986
3.0	.9987	.9987	.9987	.9988	.9988	.9989	.9989	.9989	.9990	.9990

TABLE F

Normal Distribution

AREA FROM MEAN TO Z

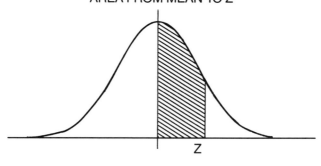

Z

Z	.00	.01	.02	.03	.04	.05	.06	.07	.08	.09
0.0	0.0000	.0040	.0080	.0120	.0160	.0199	.0239	.0279	.0319	.0359
.1	.0398	.0438	.0478	.0517	.0557	.0596	.0636	.0675	.0714	.0753
.2	.0793	.0832	.0871	.0910	.0948	.0987	.1026	.1064	.1103	.1141
.3	.1179	.1217	.1255	.1293	.1331	.1368	.1406	.1443	.1480	.1517
.4	.1554	.1591	.1628	.1664	.1700	.1736	.1772	.1808	.1844	.1879
.5	.1915	.1950	.1985	.2019	.2054	.2088	.2123	.2157	.2190	.2224
.6	.2257	.2291	.1324	.2357	.2389	.2422	.2454	.2486	.2517	.2549
.7	.2580	.2611	.2642	.2673	.2704	.2734	.2764	.2794	.2823	.2852
.8	.2881	.2910	.2939	.2967	.2995	.3023	.3051	.3078	.3106	.3133
.9	.3159	.3186	.3212	.3238	.3264	.3289	.3315	.3340	.3365	.3389
1.0	.3413	.3438	.3461	.3485	.3508	.3531	.3554	.3577	.3599	.3621
1.1	.3643	.3665	.3686	.3708	.3729	.3749	.3770	.3790	.3810	.3830
1.2	.3849	.3869	.3888	.3907	.3925	.3944	.3962	.3980	.3997	.4015
1.3	.4032	.4049	.4066	.4082	.4099	.4115	.4131	.4147	.4162	.4177
1.4	.4192	.4207	.4222	.4236	.4251	.4265	.4279	.4292	.4306	.4319
1.5	.4332	.4345	.4357	.4370	.4382	.4394	.4406	.4418	.4429	.4441
1.6	.4452	.4463	.4474	.4484	.4495	.4505	.4515	.4525	.4535	.4545
1.7	.4554	.4564	.4573	.4582	.4591	.4599	.4608	.4616	.4625	.4633
1.8	.4641	.4649	.4656	.4664	.4671	.4678	.4686	.4693	.4699	.4706
1.9	.4713	.4719	.4726	.4732	.4738	.4744	.4750	.4756	.4761	.4767
2.0	.4772	.4778	.4783	.4788	.4793	.4798	.4803	.4808	.4812	.4817
2.1	.4821	.4826	.4830	.4834	.4838	.4842	.4846	.4850	.4854	.4857
2.2	.4861	.4864	.4868	.4871	.4875	.4878	.4881	.4884	.4887	.4890
2.3	.4893	.4896	.4898	.4901	.4904	.4906	.4909	.4911	.4913	.4916
2.4	.4918	.4920	.4922	.4925	.4927	.4929	.4931	.4932	.4934	.4936
2.5	.4938	.4940	.4941	.4943	.4945	.4946	.4948	.4949	.4951	.4952
2.6	.4953	.4955	.4956	.4957	.4959	.4960	.4961	.4962	.4963	.4964
2.7	.4965	.4966	.4967	.4968	.4969	.4970	.4971	.4972	.4973	.4974
2.8	.4974	.4975	.4976	.4977	.4977	.4978	.4979	.4979	.4980	.4981
2.9	.4981	.4982	.4982	.4983	.4984	.4984	.4985	.4985	.4986	.4986
3.0	.4987	.4987	.4987	.4988	.4988	.4989	.4989	.4989	.4990	.4990

TABLE G

Normal Distribution

AREA BEYOND Z

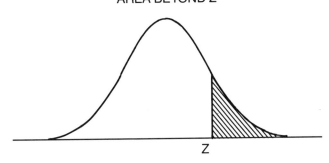

Z	.00	.01	.02	.03	.04	.05	.06	.07	.08	.09
0.0	.5000	.4960	.4920	.4880	.4840	.4801	.4761	.4721	.4681	.4641
.1	.4602	.4562	.4522	.4483	.4443	.4404	.4364	.4325	.4286	.4247
.2	.4207	.4168	.4129	.4090	.4052	.4013	.3974	.3936	.3897	.3859
.3	.3821	.3783	.3745	.3707	.3669	.3632	.3594	.3557	.3520	.3483
.4	.3446	.3481	.3372	.3336	.3300	.3264	.3228	.3192	.3156	.3121
.5	.3085	.3050	.3015	.2981	.2946	.2912	.2877	.2843	.2810	.2776
.6	.2743	.2709	.2676	.2643	.2611	.2578	.2546	.2514	.2483	.2451
.7	.2420	.2389	.2358	.2327	.2296	.2266	.2236	.2206	.2177	.2148
.8	.2119	.2090	.2061	.2033	.2005	.1977	.1949	.1922	.1894	.1867
.9	.1841	.1814	.1788	.1762	.1736	.1711	.1685	.1660	.1635	.1611
1.0	.1587	.1562	.1539	.1515	.1492	.1469	.1446	.1423	.1401	.1379
1.1	.1357	.1335	.1314	.1292	.1271	.1251	.1230	.1210	.1190	.1170
1.2	.1151	.1131	.1112	.1093	.1075	.1056	.1038	.1020	.1003	.0985
1.3	.0968	.0951	.0934	.0918	.0901	.0885	.0869	.0853	.0838	.0823
1.4	.0808	.0793	.0778	.0764	.0749	.0735	.0721	.0708	.0694	.0681
1.5	.0668	.0655	.0643	.0630	.0618	.0606	.0594	.0582	.0571	.0559
1.6	.0548	.0537	.0526	.0516	.0505	.0495	.0485	.0475	.0465	.0455
1.7	.0446	.0436	.0427	.0418	.0409	.0401	.0392	.0384	.0375	.0367
1.8	.0359	.0351	.0344	.0336	.0329	.0322	.0314	.0307	.0301	.0294
1.9	.0287	.0281	.0274	.0268	.0262	.0256	.0250	.0244	.0239	.0233
2.0	.0228	.0222	.0217	.0212	.0207	.0202	.0197	.0192	.0188	.0183
2.1	.0179	.0174	.0170	.0166	.0162	.0158	.0154	.0150	.0146	.0143
2.2	.0139	.0136	.0132	.0129	.0125	.0122	.0119	.0116	.0113	.0110
2.3	.0107	.0104	.0102	.0099	.0096	.0094	.0091	.0089	.0087	.0084
2.4	.0082	.0080	.0078	.0075	.0073	.0071	.0069	.0068	.0066	.0064
2.5	.0062	.0060	.0059	.0057	.0055	.0054	.0052	.0051	.0049	.0048
2.6	.0047	.0045	.0044	.0043	.0041	.0040	.0039	.0038	.0037	.0036
2.7	.0035	.0034	.0033	.0032	.0031	.0030	.0029	.0028	.0027	.0026
2.8	.0026	.0025	.0024	.0023	.0023	.0022	.0021	.0021	.0020	.0019
2.9	.0019	.0018	.0018	.0017	.0016	.0016	.0015	.0015	.0014	.0014
3.0	.0013	.0013	.0013	.0012	.0012	.0011	.0011	.0011	.0010	.0010

BIBLIOGRAPHY

Bazovsky I. *Reliability Theory and Practices.* Englewood Cliffs, NJ: Prentice Hall, 1963.

Burr IW. *Applied Statistical Methods.* New York, NY: Academic Press, 1974.

Ireson WG (editor). *Reliability Handbook.* New York, NY: McGraw-Hill, Inc., 1966.

Juran JM, Gryna FM. *Juran's Quality Control Handbook,* 4th ed. New York, NY: McGraw-Hill, 1988.

Kapur KC, Lamberson LR. *Reliability in Engineering Design.* New York, NY: John Wiley and Sons, Inc., 1974.

Mann NR, Schafer RE, Singpurwalla ND. *Methods for Statistical Analysis of Reliability Life.* New York, NY: John Wiley and Sons, Inc., 1974.

Nelson LS. "Upper Confidence Limits on Average Numbers of Occurrences." *Journal of Quality Technology* 21, No. 1 (January 1989): 71-72.

Practical Reliability Engineering. Philadelphia, PA: P.D.T. O'Connor, Heyden and Son, Inc., 1981.

Shooman ML. *Probabilistic Reliability: An Engineering Approach.* New York, NY: McGraw-Hill, 1968.

Yurkowski W. *Nonelectronic Reliability Handbook.* Griffis AFB, NY: Hughes Aircraft Co., 1970.

INDEX